English Pronunciation Illustrated

English
Pronunciation
Illustrated

John Trim
Director, Department of Linguistics
University of Cambridge

Drawings by
Peter Kneebone

Cambridge University Press
Cambridge
London · New York · Melbourne

Published by the Syndics of the Cambridge University Press
The Pitt Building, Trumpington Street, Cambridge CB2 1RP
Bentley House, 200 Euston Road, London NW1 2DB
32 East 57th Street, New York, NY10022, USA
296 Beaconsfield Parade, Middle Park, Melbourne 3206, Australia

Library of Congress catalogue card number: 74–25643

ISBN 0 521 20634 0

First published 1965
Reprinted 1970 1974
Second edition 1975
Reprinted 1977

Printed in Great Britain at the
University Press, Cambridge

Contents

Preface

The aim of this book is to provide teachers and learners of spoken English with practice material in an amusing form. Some suggestions for using it will be found on page 9.

The material is grouped by phonemes, starting in each case with common concrete nouns and proceeding through noun phrases to sentences. Some phrases and sentences may seem difficult at first sight. They are not designed as 'tongue-twisters' but as a basis for catenation exercises. Each contains a 'head' or 'core' phrase (normally the first) which can easily be said by itself. The whole sentence can then be built up by adding successive phrases. To facilitate the use of the book in this way, the sentences (and some longer phrases) have been subdivided by bars (|) into phrasal elements.

The vocabulary has been chosen to present the sounds of English in a variety of contexts and combinations. Special emphasis has been placed on minimal contrasts, which serve to concentrate the learner's attention on the distinctive sound features which characterise the phonemes of English. For revision and further practice a forward and reverse word index is provided, together with a comprehensive classified list of minimally contrastive word pairs.

Inevitably, some of the close-on 1500 words selected are more common than others. However, even if a number of words are not within the learner's previous vocabulary, their concrete nature and the illustrations provided should avoid any serious comprehension problems. It is not intended that the vocabulary should be memorised; its primary function is to afford phonetic practice and learners will readily accept it as such.

An account of the type of English pronunciation represented here will be found in J. D. O'Connor: *Better English Pronunciation* (CUP, 1967). Further practice material incorporating English sounds into continuous texts will be found in the same author's *Phonetic Drill Reader* (CUP, 1973).

A phonetic transcription is provided throughout, which a teacher may use for systematic teaching and to focus attention on points of difficulty. Which transcription to use is nowadays problematic. The long period of stability based on acceptance of Daniel Jones' *English Pronouncing Dictionary* is now at an end and a number of competing systems with trivial differences are again in use. Somewhat arbitrarily, the system used in A. C. Gimson, *An Introduction to the Pronunciation of English* has been employed. Little difficulty should however be experienced by learners in transferring to or from other notational systems representing the same basic phonological system.

Though primarily aimed at the foreign learner, this booklet with its visual appeal and light humour should prove useful to teachers of speech and drama and to speech therapists.

J.T.

How to use this book

Here are some suggestions for using this book. They have been made as explicit as possible for the guidance of users with little or no previous experience of pronunciation teaching. The book can however be used in many different ways and experienced teachers of spoken English will develop new ways of their own for working with it.

A Elementary class teaching

1 The teacher reads, carefully but naturally, the simple examples. (e.g. 'a tree...', 'three leaves...', 'a bee...', 'a sheep...', while the class listen.) Their attention will at this stage be largely concentrated on the picture.

2 The teacher reads the examples again. This time the pictures are covered up and the class watch the teacher's face. Their attention is thus switched to the sound and articulation of the words.

3 The examples are read a third time. This time the class look at the pictures and the wording. They thus make a preliminary and approximate association of sound, sense and written word form.

4 The teacher re-reads the first example. The pupils repeat it together. The example is read and imitated again. The second example is then read, and so on. If the group impression is correct, most individuals will benefit by comparing their immediate hearing of their own pronunciation and that of the group, to which they will tend to conform. Care must be taken however that an incorrect 'group accent' is not allowed to develop. This danger is, of course, greatest in classes composed of pupils who all have the same mother tongue.

5 Each member of the class in turn takes an example, working through them in order (so that numbers 1, 5, 9 say 'a tree', 2, 6, 10 'three leaves', etc.). The teacher should respond to any unacceptable pronunciation by repeating the model. If the pupil does not then correct his fault, it should be noted for later treatment, especially if a meaningful contrast (e.g. i:/ɪ) appears not to be observed. As a general rule, however, it does not seem advisable to lose pace by dwelling on an individual's incapacity for simple imitation. Such cases require more systematic teaching.

6 At this point, the vocabulary, being simple and concrete, can be used in simple structures for repetition, e.g. 'Here is a tree', 'Here are three leaves', 'Here is a bee', 'Here is a sheep', 'There is (are)...', 'This/that is...', 'These/those are....'. In addition such questions as 'Is this a tree?', 'Yes, it's a tree'; 'Is this a bee?', 'No, it's a sheep'; 'Which is a bee?', 'This is a bee' can be asked.

7 After dealing with the simple examples, the phrases are treated. These are best built up element by element; thus: 'a fleet... (a fleet)', 'a fleet at sea (a fleet at sea)'.

8 This building principle applies particularly to the longer sentences; thus: 'Stephen', 'Stephen meets Eve', 'Stephen meets Eve one evening', 'Stephen meets Eve one evening for a meal'. To a large extent, the sentences are designed like the example given, so that they can be built up from left to right. Sometimes a less straightforward order is required; thus on p. 15, 'a witch', 'a wicked witch', 'which is a wicked witch?', 'which of the women is a wicked witch?', 'which of the six thin women is a wicked witch?' These examples demand more of the teacher but add variety and develop a feeling for syntax.

This technique of expansion is an excellent means of developing a rhythmic sense and the skill of catenation. Pupils who collapse into a non-English rhythm, or stammer and lose all fluency when confronted by longer sentences as indigestible wholes, are delighted to find how far they can get along a sequence built up in this way.

9 The next sound is dealt with in a similar way, and so on.

Minimal pairs

A particular importance attaches to the sound contrasts (e.g. p. 16 i:/ɪ). The most important pronunciation errors are those which involve the loss of a meaningful distinction, since they easily lead to misunderstandings.

Nineteen of the sets most frequently confused by foreign learners have been included at intervals in this book.* The minimal pairs may be used in the following ways:

a First, the teacher reads each pair: sheep, ship; bean, bin; meal, mill; lead, lid.

b Secondly, each group: sheep, bean, meal, lead; ship, bin, mill, lid.

c Thirdly, the teacher reads each pair, which is imitated by the pupil. It is important, however, to realise that pupils who do not make the distinction will in all probability not hear it either, even when the contrast is apparently clearly produced in direct contrast, as above.

d In order to find out whether this is so, the teacher points to one of the pair and says, for example, 'Is this a ship?' The pupil must say Yes or No, and reveal whether he has identified the word correctly or not. A single question may of course be right by chance. However, five or six rapid questions pointing randomly between the two (e.g. R, L, L, R, L, R, or L, L, R, L, R, L, etc.) will produce a reliable answer.

Alternatively, the teacher may point to a pair and ask: 'Which is a sheep?' 'Which is a ship?' or to the group as a whole, saying: 'Show me the sheep', 'Show me the bird', 'Show me the mill', etc. Clearly these different techniques can be freely combined to prevent tedious repetition.

e Once the pupil is hearing the distinction consistently, it will still be necessary to establish the distinction in his speech. This will usually be easiest in the contrastive pairs themselves. When these are mastered, it may be advisable to go over some of the material given under the individual sounds again. Most difficulty is to be expected where the different sounds co-occur in sentences, but not as simple contrastive pairs. Practice in these is given in the longer phrases and sentences in each page of comparisons. They should be built up in the usual way (see 7 and 8 above).

* On pp. 91–6 a comprehensive list of minimally contrasting word pairs is given, drawn from the complete vocabulary of the book. These pairs are classified according to the order of phonemes in the book, and should provide ample material for practising any distinction confused by learners.

A phonetic transcription is provided for each phrase and sentence given. The modest additional effort involved in learning the symbols is well worth while.

Many pronunciation errors are due, not to the learner's inability to produce the sounds in themselves, but to a mistaken conception of the phonetic composition of words. Such errors are most easily identified by reference to a phonetic transcription. In many cases, it is only necessary for the learner to realise his error for him to be able to correct it. In any case, realisation of the proper phonetic form of the word is an indispensable pre-requisite for overcoming such 'distributional' errors – perhaps the most frequent type of error made by foreign learners.

When set out in detail, the above procedure may look long-winded, especially for a native English teacher who may not realise how difficult a task learners of English have to face. Teachers are nevertheless recommended to start off by following this method, using the humour of the material, variations in tempo within a running rhythm, and their own humanity to keep the pace lively and the lessons enjoyable.

Experienced teachers will of course make short cuts where a class is not expected to find problems, and give more practice where it is needed.

Abundant additional practice material can be drawn from the forward and reverse word indexes on pp. 84–91, and the classified list of minimal pairs on pp. 91–6.

When the material of this book has been mastered, readers are recommended to work with J. D. O'Connor's *Phonetic Drill Reader* (CUP, 1973), in which longer dialogues are skilfully based on particular sounds, contrasts and combinations.

B *Advanced classes*

With advanced students, the pages dealing with single sounds are perhaps best used quite light-heartedly for diagnostic purposes, and catenation exercises, allowing conversation to develop out of the visual humour, particularly the exploitation of British cultural stereotypes. The contrastive pairs can be used for remedial purposes as described above.

Teachers and students of English as a foreign language can have the techniques explained, and be made to see their errors objectively in terms of the interference principle, and as paradigmatic for those they will find in their own pupils.

C *Students without a teacher*

Students who have access to a native English speaker can easily follow the course outlined above for class-work by instructing the speaker to carry out the relatively straightforward actions of the teacher described. With a little practice, it should become quite easy for the native speaker to play the teacher's role, though the student cannot, of course, benefit from the skilled teacher's ability to recognise and analyse errors and to fit special remedies to special cases.

D *Students and classes without a good native speaker to act as model*

We recommend buying the cassettes or reels on which the complete material of the book is recorded. These may be used in a straightforward language laboratory if transferred to the master track. Preferably the recordings should be managed by a teacher as though a native speaker were present, in accordance with the procedure detailed above, or worked into a programmed form by editing.

E *Speech therapists and teachers of English as a mother tongue*

Adult aphasics will find the pictures, being simple but not too childish, of help in re-establishing links between concepts, sounds and spellings. The systematic sound contrasts will also be useful for work with dyslalics, and also, if so desired, in showing differences between the sound pattern of received pronunciation and the various regional pronunciations of English.

a tree   three leaves   a bee   a sheep
ə 'triː   'θriː 'liːvz   ə 'biː   ə 'ʃiːp

a fleet at sea   ice cream for tea   Stephen | meets Eve |
ə 'fliːt ət 'siː   'aɪs 'kriːm fə 'tiː   one evening | for a meal
                                         'stiːvn | miːts 'iːv |
                                         'wʌn 'iːvnɪŋ | fər ə 'miːl

Stephen | is greedy. | He eats |
three pieces | of cheese |
'stiːvn | ɪz 'griːdɪ | hɪ iːts |
'θriː 'piːsɪz | əv 'tʃiːz |

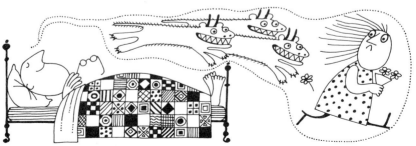

Asleep, | Stephen dreams | of Eve. | He sees Eve | fleeing | from three beasts |
ə'sliːp | 'stiːvn 'driːmz | əv 'iːv | hɪ 'siːz 'iːv | 'fliːɪŋ | frəm 'θriː 'biːsts |

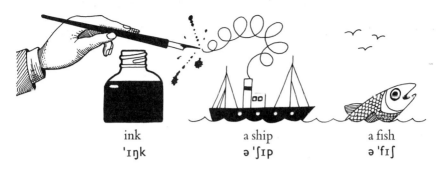

ink
'ɪŋk

a ship
ə 'ʃɪp

a fish
ə 'fɪʃ

a biscuit
ə 'bɪskɪt

a tin whistle
ə 'tɪn 'wɪsl

a big pig
ə 'bɪg 'pɪg

a little kitten
ə 'lɪtl 'kɪtn

a kitchen sink | with
dishes in it |
ə 'kɪtʃɪn 'sɪŋk | wɪð
'dɪʃɪz ɪn ɪt |

Which | of the six | thin women | is a wicked witch? |
'wɪtʃ | əv ðə 'sɪks | 'θɪn 'wɪmɪn | ɪz ə 'wɪkɪd 'wɪtʃ |

a sheep
ə ˈʃiːp

a ship
ə ˈʃɪp

a bean
ə ˈbiːn

a bin
ə ˈbɪn

a meal
ə ˈmiːl

a mill
ə ˈmɪl

a lead
ə ˈliːd

a lid
ə ˈlɪd

Jean likes gin. | . . . but gin doesn't like Jean ! |
ˈdʒiːn ˌlaɪks ˈdʒɪn | bət ˈdʒɪn ˈdʌznt ˌlaɪk ˈdʒiːn |

Sleepy Freda | seeks size
six slippers | to fit her feet |
ˈsliːpɪ ˈfriːdə | ˌsiːks ˈsaɪz
ˈsɪks ˈslɪpəz | tə ˈfɪt hɜː ˈfiːt |

Fish | and chips | are cheap |
and easy to eat |
ˈfɪʃ | ən ˈtʃɪps | ə ˈtʃiːp |
ənd ˈiːzɪ tʊ ˈiːt |

a leg
ə 'leg

a tent
ə 'tent

a penny
ə 'penɪ

a letter
ə 'letə

a wren's nest
ə 'renz ˌnest

seven pets
'sevn 'pets

a treasure chest
ə 'treʒə ˌtʃest

ten well-dressed men
'ten 'wel 'drest 'men

a wedding-dress
ə 'wedɪŋ ˌdres

eleven hens | with twelve eggs | in ten nests |
ɪ'levn 'henz | wɪð 'twelv 'egz | ɪn 'ten 'nests |

æ

a hand
ə ˈhænd

a map
ə ˈmæp

a stamp
ə ˈstæmp

a flag
ə ˈflæg

a tank
ə ˈtæŋk

a jazz band
ə ˈdʒæz ˌbænd

a fat man | clapping | his hands |
ə ˈfæt ˈmæn | ˈklæpɪŋ | ɪz ˈhændz |

a black cat | catching a fat rat |
ə ˈblæk ˈkæt | ˈkætʃɪŋ ə ˈfæt ˈræt |

Anne | has plaits | and black slacks. | Harry | has a hacking jacket
Harry and Anne | are standing | hand-in-hand |
ˈæn | hæz ˈplæts | ən ˈblæk ˈslæks | ˈhærɪ | ˌhæz ə ˈhækɪŋ ˌdʒækɪt |
ˈhærɪ ənd ˈæn | ə ˈstændɪŋ | ˈhænd ɪn ˈhænd |

a pet
ə ˈpet

a pat
ə ˈpæt

one man
ˈwʌn ˈmæn

many men
ˈmenɪ ˈmen

a net
ə ˈnet

a gnat
ə ˈnæt

pedalling
ˈpedlɪŋ

paddling
ˈpædlɪŋ

Ted | has Dad's hat | on his head |
ˈted | hæz ˈdædz ˈhæt | ɔn ɪz ˌhed |

Jack has a check
cap | in his hand |
ˈdʒæk hæz ə ˈtʃek
ˈkæp ɪn ɪz ˈhænd |

Jack's Czech friend | Franz |
is very expansive |
dʒæks ˈtʃek ˈfrend | ˈfrænts |
ɪz ˈverɪ ɪkˈspænsɪv |

Franz's French friend |
is very expensive |
ˈfræntsɪz | ˈfrentʃ | ˈfrend |
ɪz ˈverɪ ɪksˈpensɪv |

a puff
ə ˈpʌf

a cup
ə ˈkʌp

a glove
ʌ ˈglʌv

a gun	a jump	a duck
ə ˈgʌn	ə ˈdʒʌmp	ə ˈdʌk

a country cousin
ə ˈkʌntrɪ ˈkʌzn

a lovely crusty buttered bun | for supper |
ə ˈlʌvlɪ ˈkrʌstɪ ˈbʌtəd ˈbʌn | fə ˈsʌpə |

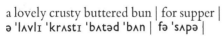

Cuthbert | puts some mustard |
in his Mother's custard |
ˈkʌθbət | ˌpʊts səm ˈmʌstəd |
ɪn ɪz ˈmʌðəz ˈkʌstəd |

a thump
ə ˈθʌmp

Cuthbert's young brother | wonders why Mother | doesn't love her other son |
ˈkʌθbəts ˈjʌŋ ˈbrʌðə | ˈwʌndəz | waɪ ˈmʌðə ˈdʌznt ˈlʌv hɜr ˈʌðə ˈsʌn |

a hat	a hut	a battler	a butler
ə ˈhæt	ə ˈhʌt	ə ˈbætlə	ə ˈbʌtlə

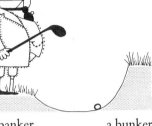

a stamp	a stump	a banker	a bunker
ə ˈstæmp	ə ˈstʌmp	ə ˈbæŋkə	ə ˈbʌŋkə

These windows were shattered
ˈðiːz ˈwɪndəuz wə ˈʃætəd

These windows were shuttered
ˈðiːz ˈwɪndəuz wə ˈʃʌtəd

mashed potatoes with butter
ˈmæʃt pəˈteɪtəuz wɪð ˈbʌtə

mushed potatoes with batter
ˈmʌʃt pəˈteɪtəuz wɪð ˈbætə

a heart
ə ˈhɑːt

a harp
ə ˈhɑːp

an arm
ən ˈɑːm

a mast
ə ˈmɑːst

a bard
ə ˈbɑːd

a castle
ə ˈkɑːsl

a palm
ə ˈpɑːm

a carpet
ə ˈkɑːpɪt

a fast car
ə ˈfɑːst ˈkɑː

a farm-cart
ə ˈfɑːmˌkɑːt

a dark barn | in a large farm-yard |
ə ˈdɑːk ˈbɑːn | ɪn ə ˈlɑːdʒ ˈfɑːmˌjɑːd |

Mark | can't park | his car | in the barn | because of a calf | and a
large cart | blocking the farm-yard |
ˈmɑːk | ˈkɑːnt ˈpɑːk | hɪz ˈkɑːr | ɪn ðə ˈbɑːn | bɪkɒz əv ə ˈkɑːf | ənd ə
ˈlɑːdʒ ˈkɑːt | ˈblɒkɪŋ ðə ˈfɑːmˌjɑːd |

a park
ə ˈpɑːk

a puck
ə ˈpʌk

a carp
ə ˈkɑːp

a cup
ə ˈkʌp

a larva
ə ˈlɑːvə

a lover
ə ˈlʌvə

a barking dog
ə ˈbɑːkɪŋ ˈdɒg

a bucking horse
ə ˈbʌkɪŋ ˈhɔːs

| a dog
ə ˈdɒg | a fog
ə ˈfɒg | a blot
ə ˈblɒt | a chop
ə ˈtʃɒp | a shop
ə ˈʃɒp |

a lot of knots
ə ˈlɒt əv ˈnɒts

a dog squatting on a rotten log
ə ˈdɒg ˈskwɒtɪŋ ɒn ə ˈrɒtn ˈlɒg

John
ˈdʒɒn

Olive
ˈɒlɪv

John is strong
ˈdʒɒn ɪz ˈstrɒŋ

Olive is not
ˈɒlɪv ɪz ˈnɒt

John is a docker
ˈdʒɒn ɪz ə ˈdɒkə

Olive is a shopper
ˈɒlɪv ɪz ə ˈʃɒpə

Olive | watches John | load a locked strong-box | on a yacht | in a lock |
at the docks |
ˈɒlɪv | ˈwɒtʃɪz ˈdʒɒn | ˈləʊd ə ˈlɒkt ˈstrɒŋ-ˌbɒks | ɒn ə ˈjɒt | ɪn ə ˈlɒk |
ət ðə ˈdɒks |

a dun	a don	a hug	a hog
ə 'dʌn	ə 'dɒn	ə 'hʌg	ə 'hɒg

a suck	a sock	a buddy	a body
ə 'sʌk	ə 'sɒk	ə 'bʌdɪ	ə 'bɒdɪ

The zoologist | wonders | about bugs. | The botanist | wanders | about bogs |
ðə zəʊ'ɒlədʒɪst | 'wʌndəz | əbaʊt 'bʌgz | ðə 'bɒtənɪst | 'wɒndəz | əbaʊt 'bɒgz |

a darn
ə ˈdɑːn

a don
ə ˈdɒn

a tart
ə ˈtɑːt

a tot
ə ˈtɒt

a shark
ə ˈʃɑːk

a shock
ə ˈʃɒk

a Rajah
ə ˈrɑːdʒə

Roger
ˈrɒdʒə

CLUMPING 10
VIA MURK

CLUMPING 10
VIA GRIST

TRESPASSE
WILL BE
PROSECUTE

This cross-country runner is last . | This cross-country runner is lost |
ˈðɪs ˌkrɒs-ˈkʌntrɪ ˌrʌnər ɪz ˈlɑːst | ˈðɪs ˌkrɒs-ˌkʌntrɪ ˌrʌnər ɪz ˈlɒst |

a thought
ə ˈθɔːt

a talk
ə ˈtɔːk

a yawn
ə ˈjɔːn

a call
ə ˈkɔːl

a walk
ə ˈwɔːk

a stormy dawn
ə ˈstɔːmɪ ˈdɔːn

Paul
ˈpɔːl

Maud
ˈmɔːd

Maud is short
ˈmɔːd ɪz ˈʃɔːt

Paul is tall
ˈpɔːl ɪz ˈtɔːl

Maud | is walking | on the lawn. | Paul | is crawling | along a wall |
Maud warns Paul | 'You'll fall!' | 'Not at all!' | retorts Paul |
ˈmɔːd | ɪz ˈwɔːkɪŋ | ɒn ðə ˈlɔːn | ˈpɔːl | ɪz ˈkrɔːlɪŋ | əlɒŋ ə ˈwɔːl |
ˈmɔːd ˈwɔːnz ˈpɔːl | juːl ˈfɔːl | nɒt ə ˈtɔːl | rɪˌtɔːts ˌpɔːl |

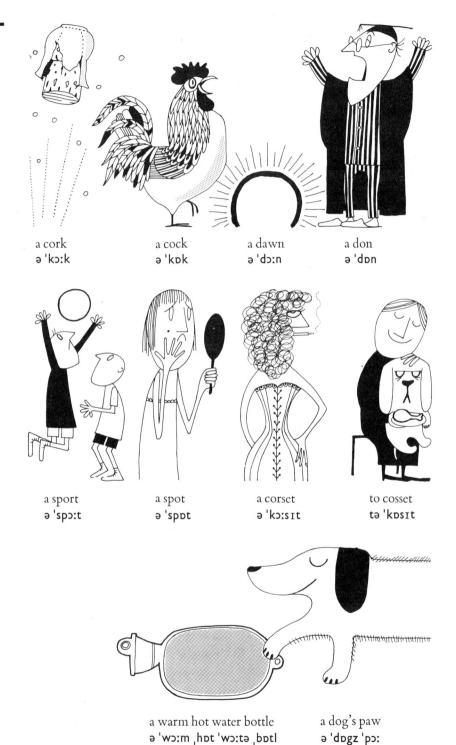

a cork
ə ˈkɔːk

a cock
ə ˈkɒk

a dawn
ə ˈdɔːn

a don
ə ˈdɒn

a sport
ə ˈspɔːt

a spot
ə ˈspɒt

a corset
ə ˈkɔːsɪt

to cosset
tə ˈkɒsɪt

a warm hot water bottle
ə ˌwɔːm ˌhɒt ˈwɔːtə ˌbɒtl

a dog's paw
ə ˈdɒgz ˈpɔː

a wood
ə ˈwʊd

a butcher
ə ˈbʊtʃə

a cook
ə ˈkʊk

a bull
ə ˈbʊl

a rook
ə ˈrʊk

The cook looks at her cookery-book
ðə ˈkʊk ˈlʊks ət ɜː ˈkʊkərɪ ˌbʊk

She puts some sugar in the pudding
ʃɪ ˈpʊts səm ˈʃʊgər ɪn ðə ˈpʊdɪŋ

The pudding looks good
ðə ˈpʊdɪŋ ˌlʊks ˈgʊd

Look | at Luke, | pulling a poor fool
out of the pool | in the wood |
ˈlʊk | ət ˈluːk | ˈpʊlɪŋ ə ˈpʊə ˈfuːl |
aʊt əv ðə ˈpuːl | ɪn ðə ˈwʊd |

This foolish, bookish Duke | is too
full | of good food | to move | a foot |
ðɪs ˈfuːlɪʃ ˈbʊkɪʃ ˈdjuːk | ɪz ˈtuː
ˈfʊl | əv ˈgʊd ˈfuːd | tə ˈmuːv | ə ˈfʊt |

a new moon
ə ˈnjuː ˈmuːn

a rude uncouth youth
ə ˈruːd ˈʌnkuːθ ˈjuːθ

a brute
ə ˈbruːt

a goose
ə ˈguːs

a stool
ə ˈstuːl

two new shoes
ˈtuː ˈnjuː ˈʃuːz

a few used boots
ə ˈfjuː ˈjuːzd ˈbuːts

Hugh
ˈhjuː

Sue
ˈsuː

Hugh's tooth is loose
ˈhjuːz ˈtuːθ ɪz ˈluːs

Sue is beautiful
ˈsuː ɪz ˈbjuːtɪfl

Hugh | shoots | a moose | and loses his loose tooth |
ˈhjuː | ˈʃuːts | ə ˈmuːs | ənd ˈluːzɪz ɪz ˈluːs ˈtuːθ |

Sue | is foolish | and stupid | at school | as a rule |
ˈsuː | ɪz ˈfuːlɪʃ | ən ˈstjuːpɪd | ət ˈskuːl | əz ə ˈruːl |

Myrtle
'mɜːtl

her purse	her curl	her jersey	her skirt
hɜː 'pɜːs	hɜː 'kɜːl	hɜː 'dʒɜːzɪ	hɜː 'skɜːt

a dirty turtle
ə 'dɜːtɪ 'tɜːtl

an early bird | with a squirming earth-worm |
ən 'ɜːlɪ 'bɜːd | wɪð ə 'skwɜːmɪŋ 'ɜːθ-ˌwɜːm |

a serpent | lurking |
amid the ferns |
ə 'sɜːpənt | 'lɜːkɪŋ |
əmɪd ðə 'fɜːnz |

Pearl
'pɜːl

Pearl is a circus girl
'pɜːl ɪz ə 'sɜːkəs ˌgɜːl

An earl | gave Pearl a fur | and a circlet | of pearls | for her thirty-first birthday |
ən 'ɜːl | geɪv 'pɜːl ə 'fɜː | ənd ə 'sɜːklɪt | əv 'pɜːlz | fə hɜː 'θɜːtɪ 'fɜːst 'bɜːθdeɪ |

a balloon
ə bə'luːn

a banana
ə bə'nɑːnə

a cactus
ə 'kæktəs

a cormorant
ə 'kɔːmərənt

an abacus
ən 'æbəkəs

a fashionable photographer
ə 'fæʃənəbl fə'tɒgrəfə

an adventurous professor
ən əd'ventʃərəs prə'fesə

an amateur astrologer
ən 'æmətər ə'strɒlədʒə

a professional astronomer
ə prə'feʃənl ə'strɒnəmə

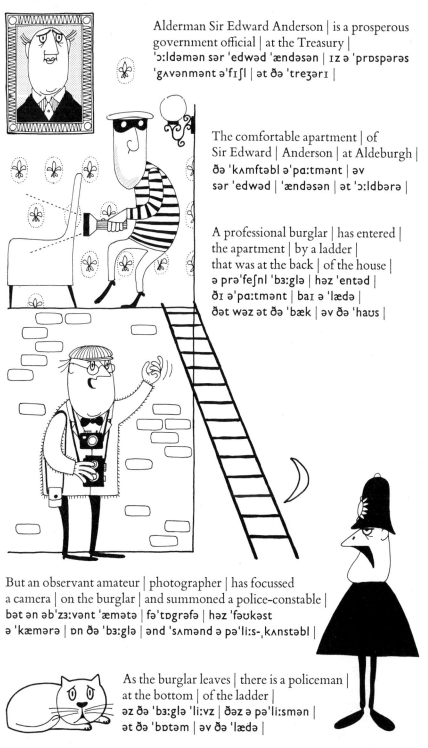

Alderman Sir Edward Anderson | is a prosperous
government official | at the Treasury |
'ɔːldəmən sər 'edwəd 'ændəsən | ɪz ə 'prɒspərəs
'gʌvənmənt əˈfɪʃl | ət ðə 'treʒərɪ |

The comfortable apartment | of
Sir Edward | Anderson | at Aldeburgh |
ðə 'kʌmftəbl əˈpɑːtmənt | əv
sər 'edwəd | 'ændəsən | ət 'ɔːldbərə |

A professional burglar | has entered |
the apartment | by a ladder |
that was at the back | of the house |
ə prəˈfeʃnl 'bɜːglə | həz 'entəd |
ðɪ əˈpɑːtmənt | baɪ ə 'lædə |
ðət wəz ət ðə 'bæk | əv ðə 'haʊs |

But an observant amateur | photographer | has focussed
a camera | on the burglar | and summoned a police-constable |
bət ən əbˈzɜːvənt 'æmətə | fəˈtɒgrəfə | həz 'fəʊkəst
ə 'kæmərə | ɒn ðə 'bɜːglə | ənd 'sʌmənd ə pəˈliːs-ˌkʌnstəbl |

As the burglar leaves | there is a policeman |
at the bottom | of the ladder |
əz ðə 'bɜːglə 'liːvz | ðəz ə pəˈliːsmən |
ət ðə 'bɒtəm | əv ðə 'lædə |

eɪ

a space-ship
ə 'speɪsˌʃɪp

a baby whale
ə 'beɪbɪ 'weɪl

a sailor
ə 'seɪlə

a mate
ə 'meɪt

a great wave
ə 'greɪt 'weɪv

daybreak
'deɪˌbreɪk

a grey, rainy day
ə 'greɪ, 'reɪnɪ 'deɪ

a train | waiting | at a railway station |
ə 'treɪn | 'weɪtɪŋ | ət ə 'reɪlweɪ ˌsteɪʃn |

James | plays | with
trains | and planes. |
'dʒeɪmz | 'pleɪz | wɪð
'treɪnz | ənd 'pleɪnz |

Jane | bakes | eight
cakes |
'dʒeɪn | 'beɪks | 'eɪt
'keɪks |

James
'dʒeɪmz

Jane
'dʒeɪn

James | takes a cake |
from Jane's plate |
'dʒeɪmz | 'teɪks ə 'keɪk |
frəm 'dʒeɪnz 'pleɪt |

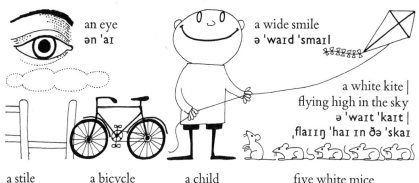

an eye
ən 'aɪ

a wide smile
ə 'waɪd 'smaɪl

a white kite |
flying high in the sky
ə 'waɪt 'kaɪt |
ˌflaɪɪŋ 'haɪ ɪn ðə 'skaɪ

a stile
ə 'staɪl

a bicycle
ə 'baɪsɪkl

a child
ə 'tʃaɪld

five white mice
'faɪv 'waɪt 'maɪs

Clive
'klaɪv

Dinah
'daɪnə

Clive | climbs | high spires | at night |
'klaɪv | 'klaɪmz | 'haɪ 'spaɪəz | ət 'naɪt|

Dinah | is quite nice, |
but frightfully shy |
'daɪnə | ɪz 'kwaɪt 'naɪs |
bət 'fraɪtfəlɪ 'ʃaɪ |

Clive | decides | to invite Dinah |
to dine. | He tries to find a fine
white wine |
'klaɪv | dɪ'saɪdz | tʊ ɪn'vaɪt 'daɪnə |
tə 'daɪn |hɪ 'traɪz tə 'faɪnd ə 'faɪn
'waɪt 'waɪn |

Dinah | decides | she would like to dine |
with Clive | and arrives | on time, |
but politely declines | the white wine |
'daɪnə | dɪ'saɪdz | ʃɪd 'laɪk tə 'daɪn |
wɪð 'klaɪv, | ənd ə'raɪvz | ɒn 'taɪm, |
bət pə'laɪtlɪ dɪ'klaɪnz | ðə 'waɪt 'waɪn |

Mr Hoyle
ˈmɪstə ˈhɔɪl

a boy
ə ˈbɔɪ

a quoit
ə ˈkɔɪt

soil
ˈsɔɪl

Mr Hoyle | toils | with the soil |
ˈmɪstə ˈhɔɪl | ˈtɔɪlz | wɪð ðə ˈsɔɪl |

The boy | is adroit | with his quoit |
ðə ˈbɔɪ | ɪz əˈdrɔɪt | wɪð ɪz ˈkɔɪt |

a choice, moist oyster
ə ˈtʃɔɪs, ˈmɔɪst ˈɔɪstə

a loyal royalist
ə ˈlɔɪəl ˈrɔɪəlɪst

Roy
ˈrɔɪ

Joyce
ˈdʒɔɪs

Roy | is a noisy boy |
ˈrɔɪ | ɪz ə ˈnɔɪzɪ ˌbɔɪ |

Joyce | is spoilt | and coy |
ˈdʒɔɪs | ɪz ˈspɔɪlt | ənd ˈkɔɪ |

Joyce | enjoys annoying | Roy |
ˈdʒɔɪs | ɪnˈdʒɔɪz əˈnɔɪɪŋ | ˈrɔɪ |

Roy destroys Joyce's choicest toys
ˈrɔɪ dɪˈstrɔɪz ˈdʒɔɪsɪz ˈtʃɔɪsɪst ˈtɔɪz

a taste
ə 'teɪst

a test
ə 'test

a sailor
ə 'seɪlə

a seller
ə 'selə

they raced
'ðeɪ 'reɪst

I rest
'aɪ 'rest

David failed his exam...
'deɪvɪd 'feɪld ɪz ɪg'zæm...

so he felled the examiner!
səʊ hiː 'feld ðɪ ɪg'zæmɪnə!

Jane sails boats
'dʒeɪn 'seɪlz 'bəʊts

Jen sells boots
'dʒen 'selz 'buːts

37

to lay
tə 'leɪ

to lie
tə 'laɪ

a pain
ə 'peɪn

a pine
ə 'paɪn

hate
'heɪt

height
'haɪt

the lake that I like
ðə 'leɪk ðət aɪ 'laɪk

David baits his hook...
'deɪvɪd 'beɪts ɪz 'hʊk...

and a whiting bites it
ənd ə 'waɪtɪŋ 'baɪts ɪt

38

good boys
'gʊd 'bɔɪz

goodbyes
'gʊd 'baɪz

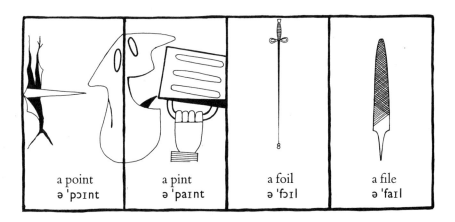

a point	a pint	a foil	a file
ə 'pɔɪnt	ə 'paɪnt	ə 'fɔɪl	ə 'faɪl

Joyce walks off with poise
'dʒɔɪs ˌwɔːks 'ɔf wɪð 'pɔɪz

Giles walks off with pies
'dʒaɪlz ˌwɔːks 'ɔf wɪð 'paɪz

a goat
ə ˈgəʊt

a cone
ə ˈkəʊn

a rose
ə ˈrəʊz

a note
ə ˈnəʊt

an overcoat
ən ˈəʊvəkəʊt

poached eggs on toast
ˈpəʊtʃt ˈegz ɒn ˈtəʊst

an old coastal boat
ən ˈəʊld ˈkəʊstəl ˈbəʊt

Joan
ˈdʒəʊn

Joe
ˈdʒəʊ

Joan | is combing | her golden hair |
ˈdʒəʊn | ɪz ˈkəʊmɪŋ | ɜː ˈgəʊldən ˈhɛə |

Joe has a noble, Roman nose |
ˈdʒəʊ hæz ə ˈnəʊbl ˈrəʊmən ˈnəʊz |

Joe | and Joan | go for a stroll. |
Joe | shows Joan his roses |
ˈdʒəʊ | ən ˈdʒəʊn | ˈgəʊ fər ə ˈstrəʊl |
ˈdʒəʊ | ˈʃəʊz ˈdʒəʊn ɪz ˈrəʊzɪz |

Joan | won't go home | alone, |
so Joe goes home | with Joan |
ˈdʒəʊn | ˈwəʊnt ˌgəʊ ˈhəʊm | əˈləʊn |
səʊ ˈdʒəʊ ˌgəʊz ˈhəʊm | ˈwɪð ˌdʒəʊn |

40

a scowl
ə ˈskaʊl

a cloud
ə ˈklaʊd

a cow
ə ˈkaʊ

a scout
ə ˈskaʊt

a plough
ə ˈplaʊ

a rout
ə ˈraʊt

This owl | has found a brown mouse | on the ground |
ðɪs ˈaʊl | əz ˈfaʊnd ə ˈbraʊn ˈmaʊs | ɒn ðə ˈgraʊnd |

a hound | with a grouse | in its mouth |
ə ˈhaʊnd | wɪd ə ˈgraʊs | ɪn ɪts ˈmaʊθ |

proud
ˈpraʊd

cowed
ˈkaʊd

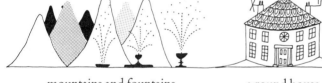

mountains and fountains
ˈmaʊntənz ənd ˈfaʊntənz

a round house
ə ˈraʊnd ˈhaʊs

The loud shouts | and howls | of the crowd | of louts | from the town | drown the sound | of the vows | of the devout | on the mound |
ðə ˈlaʊd ˈʃaʊts | ənd ˈhaʊlz | əv ðə ˈkraʊd | əv ˈlaʊts | frəm ðə ˈtaʊn | ˈdraʊn ðə ˈsaʊnd | əv ðə ˈvaʊz | əv ðə dɪˈvaʊt | ɒn ðə ˈmaʊnd |

a phone	a faun	a load	a lord
ə ˈfəʊn	ə ˈfɔːn	ə ˈləʊd	ə ˈlɔːd

a stoker	a stalker
ə ˈstəʊkə	ə ˈstɔːkə

John | has bought his adoring daughter Joan |
a motor-boat | with an outboard motor |
ˈdʒɒn | əz ˈbɔːt ɪz əˈdɔːrɪŋ ˈdɔːtə ˈdʒəʊn |
ə ˈməʊtə-ˌbəʊt | wɪð ən ˈaʊtbɔːd ˈməʊtə |

42

coals
'kəʊlz

curls
'kɜːlz

a joke
ə 'dʒəʊk

a jerk
ə 'dʒɜːk

floating
'fləʊtɪŋ

flirting
'flɜːtɪŋ

errr...

oh!

oooh!

a hope
ə 'həʊp

a hoop
ə 'huːp

a roller
ə 'rəʊlə

a ruler
ə 'ruːlə

a goal
ə 'gəʊl

a ghoul
ə 'guːl

a bow
ə ˈbəʊ

a bow
ə ˈbaʊ

a crone
ə ˈkrəʊn

a crown
ə ˈkraʊn

a foal
ə ˈfəʊl

a fowl
ə ˈfaʊl

a cold figure
ə ˈkəʊld ˌfɪɡə

a cowled figure
ə ˈkaʊld ˌfɪɡə

a spire
ə ˈspaɪə

a higher spire
ə ˈhaɪə ˈspaɪə

we conspire
wiː kənˈspaɪə

a fire
ə ˈfaɪə

a tyre
ə ˈtaɪə

some wire
səm ˈwaɪə

a towel
ə ˈtaʊəl

a tower
ə ˈtaʊə

our | shower in a flowery bower |
aʊə ˈʃaʊə | ɪn ə ˈflaʊərɪ ˈbaʊə |

Howard | is a coward, | says Brian |
ˈhaʊəd | ɪz ə ˈkaʊəd | sez ˌbraɪən |

Brian | is a liar, | says Howard |
ˈbraɪən | ɪz ə ˈlaɪə | sez ˌhaʊəd |

Brian | glowers | sourly | at Howard |
ˈbraɪən | ˈglaʊəz | ˈsaʊəlɪ | ət ˈhaʊəd |

45

a seer	a spear	fear	a deer	a tear
ə ˈsɪə	ə ˈspɪə	ˈfɪə	ə ˈdɪə	ə ˈtɪə

a theatre
ə ˈθɪətə

A dreary peer | sneers |
in the grand tier |
ə ˈdrɪərɪ ˈpɪə | ˈsnɪəz |
ɪn ðə ˈgrænd ˈtɪə |

At the rear |
they hear | the peer | and jeer |
ət ðə ˈrɪə
| ðeɪ ˈhɪə | ðə ˈpɪər | ən ˈdʒɪə |

But here, clearly
the cheers for the hero are really
fierce
bət ˈhɪə ˈklɪəlɪ
ðə ˈtʃɪəz fə ðə ˈhɪərəʊ ə ˈrɪəlɪ
ˈfɪəs

The weary hero |
[King Lear] |
is nearly in tears |
ðə ˈwɪərɪ ˈhɪərəʊ |
[ˈkɪŋ ˈlɪə] |
ɪz ˈnɪəlɪ ɪn ˈtɪəz |

tear	swear	share	despair
'tɛə	'swɛə	'ʃɛə	dɪ'spɛə

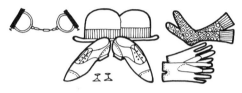

various pairs of things to wear
'vɛərɪəs 'pɛəz əv 'θɪŋz tə 'wɛə

Mary
'mɛərɪ

Mary is scared | of fairies | in the dairy |
'mɛərɪ ɪz 'skɛəd | əv 'fɛərɪz | ɪn ðə 'dɛərɪ |

Sarah
'sɛərə

Sarah has fair hair
'sɛərə hæz 'fɛə 'hɛə

Fair-haired Sarah | stares | warily | at the hairy bear, | glaring from his lair |
'fɛə-'hɛəd 'sɛərə | 'stɛəz | 'wɛərɪlɪ | ət ðə 'hɛərɪ 'bɛə | 'glɛərɪŋ frəm ɪz 'lɛə |

a spoor	a skua	fuel	a duel
ə ˈspʊə	ə ˈskjʊə	ˈfjʊəl	ə ˈdjʊəl

a poor curate
ə ˈpʊə ˈkjʊərət

a dour, cruel, furious boor
ə ˈdʊə ˈkrʊəl ˈfjʊəriəs ˈbʊə

curious tourists | with their courier |
ˈkjʊəriəs ˈtʊərɪsts | wɪð ðɛə ˈkʊəriə |
A lurid mural | is sure to lure | curious tourists |
ə ˈljʊərɪd ˈmjʊərəl | ɪz ˈʃʊə tə ˈljʊə | ˈkjʊəriəs ˈtʊərɪsts |

a lurid mural
ə ˈljʊərɪd ˈmjʊərəl

48

a pimple
ə ˈpɪmpl

a pipe
ə ˈpaɪp

a pearl pin
ə ˈpɜːl ˈpɪn

a pork pie
ə ˈpɔːk ˈpaɪ

a paper plate
ə ˈpeɪpə ˈpleɪt

a paper
ə ˈpeɪpə

a passport
ə ˈpɑːspɔːt

a pre-packed picnic
ə ˈpriːˈpækt ˈpɪknɪk

people
ˈpiːpl

a puppy
ə ˈpʌpɪ

portrait of a plump, prosperous, purposeful passenger
ˈpɔːtreɪt əv ə ˈplʌmp, ˈprɒspərəs, ˈpɜːpəsfl ˈpæsɪndʒə

Pretty Polly | Perkins |
has a pair of pretty plaits |
ˈprɪtɪ pɒlɪ | ˈpɜːkɪnz |
hæz ə ˈpɛər əv ˈprɪtɪ ˈplæts |

Pat | peeps at Pip |
playing | the piano |
ˈpæt | ˈpiːps ət ˈpɪp |
ˈpleɪɪŋ | ðə pɪˈænəʊ |

b

a bow	a bible	a baboon	a suburb
ə ˈbaʊ	ə ˈbaɪbl	ə bəˈbuːn	ə ˈsʌbɜːb

Bessie | the buxom barmaid | bringing
a bottle | of best brown | beer | from the bar |
at the back | of the 'Bull | and Bush' |
ˈbesɪ | ðə ˈbʌksm ˈbɑːmeɪd | ˌbrɪŋɪŋ
ə ˈbɒtl | əv ˈbest ˈbraʊn | ˈbɪə | frəm ðə ˈbɑː |
ət ðə bæk | əv ðə ˈbʊl | ən ˈbʊʃ |

Barbara | is a beautiful blonde | with bright blue eyes | Barbara | is bathing |
blissfully | in a bubble-bath |
ˈbɑːbərə | ɪz ə ˈbjuːtɪfl ˈblɒnd | wɪð ˈbraɪt ˈbluː ˈaɪz | ˈbɑːbərə | ɪz ˈbeɪðɪŋ |
ˈblɪsfəlɪ | ɪn ə ˈbʌbl-ˌbɑːθ |
Barbara's baby | brother | Bobby | is bouncing | a big beach-ball |
ˈbɑːbərəz ˈbeɪbɪ | ˈbrʌðə | ˈbɒbɪ | ɪz ˈbaʊnsɪŋ | ə ˈbɪg ˈbiːtʃ-ˌbɔːl |

a large pack
ə ˈlɑːdʒ ˈpæk

a large back
ə ˈlɑːdʒ ˈbæk

a poppy
ə ˈpɒpɪ

a bobby
ə ˈbɒbɪ

a big pig
ə ˈbɪg ˈpɪg

people praying
ˈpiːpl ˈpreɪɪŋ

asses braying
ˈæsɪz ˈbreɪɪŋ

A bold spy | put a big bomb | in a pork pie |
ə ˈbəʊld ˈspaɪ | ˌpʊt ə ˈbɪg ˈbɒm | ɪn ə ˈpɔːk ˈpaɪ |

The pork pie | blew up | a politician | with a big bang | in a public bar |
ðə ˈpɔːk ˈpaɪ | ˈbluː ˈʌp | ə pɒlɪ ˈtɪʃn | wɪð ə ˈbɪg ˈbæŋ | ɪn ə ˈpʌblɪk ˈbɑː |

t

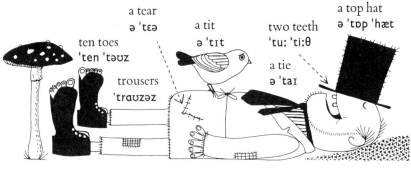

a tear
ə ˈtɛə

a tit
ə ˈtɪt

two teeth
ˈtuː ˈtiːθ

a top hat
ə ˈtɒp ˈhæt

a tie
ə ˈtaɪ

ten toes
ˈten ˈtəʊz

trousers
ˈtraʊzəz

a toadstool
ə ˈtəʊdstuːl

a tired tramp
ə ˈtaɪəd ˈtræmp

eight tall trees
ˈeɪt ˈtɔːl ˈtriːz

a tottering tower
ə ˈtɒtərɪŋ ˈtaʊə

a tattered straw hat
ə ˈtætəd ˈstrɔː ˈhæt

two terrible twins
ˈtuː ˈterɪbl ˈtwɪnz

a tea tray | with toast, | tarts and a pot |
of hot strong tea | to tempt the twins |
ə ˈtiː ˌtreɪ | wɪð ˈtəʊst | ˈtɑːts ənd ə ˈpɒt |
əv ˈhɒt ˈstrɒŋ ˈtiː | tə ˈtempt ðə ˈtwɪnz |

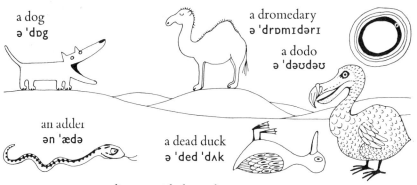

a dog
ə ˈdɒg

a dromedary
ə ˈdrɒmɪdərɪ

a dodo
ə ˈdəʊdəʊ

an adder
ən ˈædə

a dead duck
ə ˈded ˈdʌk

a distant, arid, dusty desert
ə ˈdɪstənt, ˈærɪd, ˈdʌstɪ ˈdezət

Deirdre | is the dowdy daughter |
of the Duke | of Dundas |
ˈdɪədrɪ | ɪz ðə ˈdaʊdɪ ˈdɔːtə |
əv ðə ˈdjuːk | əv ˈdʌndəs |

Deirdre is dreaming |
a dreadful dream |
ˈdɪədrɪ ɪz ˈdriːmɪŋ |
ə ˈdredfl ˈdriːm |

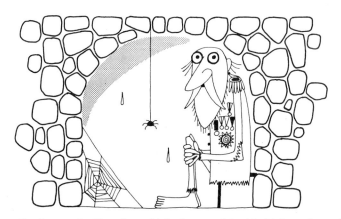

She dreams | of her dear old darling Daddy, | held deep down | in a
dark, dank, dirty dungeon, | doomed to die | on her wedding day |
ʃɪ ˈdriːmz | əv hɜː ˈdɪər əʊld ˈdɑːlɪŋ ˈdædɪ | held ˈdiːp ˈdaʊn | ɪn ə
ˈdɑːk ˈdæŋk ˈdɜːtɪ ˈdʌndʒn | ˈduːmd tə ˈdaɪ | ɒn hɜː ˈwedɪŋ ˌdeɪ |

k

a crown
ə ˈkraʊn

a cake
ə ˈkeɪk

a crumpet
ə ˈkrʌmpɪt

crockery
ˈkrɒkərɪ

a king	The cake is like a rock !	the cook who baked the cake
ə ˈkɪŋ	ðə ˈkeɪk ɪz ˌlaɪk ə ˈrɒk	ðə ˈkʊk huː ˈbeɪkt ðə ˈkeɪk

Ken quite likes Kate. |
Kate doesn't care | for Ken |
ˈken ˈkwaɪt ˈlaɪks ˈkeɪt |
ˈkeɪt ˈdʌznt ˈkɛə | fə ˈken |

Ken catches Kate |
and kisses her | quickly |
ˈken ˈkætʃɪz ˈkeɪt |
ən ˈkɪsɪz ɜː | ˈkwɪklɪ |

Kate cries, | kicks and screams. |
Ken cowers | in the corner |
ˈkeɪt ˈkraɪz | ˈkɪks ən ˈskriːmz |
ˈken ˈkaʊəz | ɪn ðə ˈkɔːnə |

Ken cures Kate | with a quick
cup | of coffee | and a cream cake |
ˈken ˈkjʊəz ˈkeɪt | wɪð ə ˈkwɪk
ˈkʌp | əv ˈkɒfɪ | ənd ə ˈkriːm ˈkeɪk |

a guide
ə 'gaɪd

a gargoyle
ə 'gaːgɔɪl

a glass
ə 'glaːs

an ogre
ən 'əʊgə

The guide gazes at the gargoyle
ðə 'gaɪd 'geɪzɪz ət ðə 'gaːgɔɪl

The ogre gargles with gusto
ðɪ 'əʊgə 'gaːglz wɪð 'gʌstəʊ

a girl guide | giggling |
at a glum guardsman |
guarding the gates |
ə 'gɜːl 'gaɪd | 'gɪglɪŋ |
ət ə 'glʌm 'gaːdzmən |
'gaːdɪŋ ðə 'geɪts |

A garden | overgrown
with grass | and gorse |
is no good | for guests |
ə 'gaːdn | 'əʊvə'grəʊn
wɪð 'graːs | ən 'gɔːs |
ɪz 'nəʊ 'gʊd | fə 'gests |

tʃ

a chubby child
ə ˈtʃʌbɪ ˈtʃaɪld

a chair
ə ˈtʃɛə

a church
ə ˈtʃɜːtʃ

an arch
ən ˈɑːtʃ

a watch-chain and watch
ə ˈwɒtʃ-ˌtʃeɪn ənd ˈwɒtʃ

Charles scratching his itching chin
ˈtʃɑːlz ˈskrætʃɪŋ ɪz ˈɪtʃɪŋ ˈtʃɪn

Charles is a cheerful chicken-farmer
ˈtʃɑːlz ɪz ə ˈtʃɪəfl ˈtʃɪkɪn-ˌfɑːmə

A poacher | is watching | Charles's chickens, | choosing which to snatch |
He chuckles | at the chance | of a choice chicken | to chew | for his lunch |
ə ˈpəʊtʃər | ɪz ˈwɒtʃɪŋ | ˈtʃɑːlzɪz ˈtʃɪkɪnz | ˈtʃuːzɪŋ ˈwɪtʃ tə ˈsnætʃ |
hɪ ˈtʃʌklz | ət ðə ˈtʃɑːns | əv ə ˈtʃɔɪs ˈtʃɪkɪn | tə ˈtʃuː | fər ɪz ˈlʌntʃ |

But the chuckle reaches Charles, |
who chases the poacher | and catches him |
bət ðə ˈtʃʌkl ˈriːtʃɪz ˈtʃɑːlz |
huː ˈtʃeɪsɪz ðə ˈpəʊtʃər | ən ˈkætʃɪz ɪm |

56

a jelly
ə ˈdʒelɪ

a juicy orange
ə ˈdʒuːsɪ ˈɒrɪndʒ

a large jug
ə ˈlɑːdʒ ˈdʒʌg

gingerbread
ˈdʒɪndʒəbred

a jam-jar
ə ˈdʒæmˌdʒɑː

Jeremy Jones
ˈdʒerəmɪ ˈdʒəʊnz

an aged judge
ən ˈeɪdʒɪd ˈdʒʌdʒ

a jolly jury
ə ˈdʒɒlɪ ˈdʒʊərɪ

The aged judge | urges the jury | to be just | but generous |
ðɪ ˈeɪdʒɪd ˈdʒʌdʒ | ˈɜːdʒɪz ðə ˈdʒʊərɪ | tə bɪ ˈdʒʌst | bət ˈdʒenərəs |

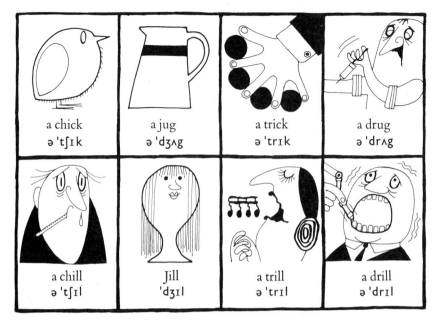

a chick ə ˈtʃɪk	a jug ə ˈdʒʌg
a trick ə ˈtrɪk	a drug ə ˈdrʌg
a chill ə ˈtʃɪl	Jill ˈdʒɪl
a trill ə ˈtrɪl	a drill ə ˈdrɪl

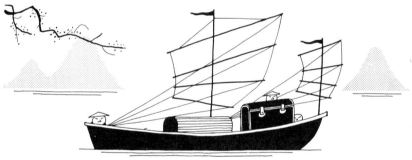

a huge treasure-chest | on a large Chinese junk |
ə ˈhjuːdʒ ˈtreʒə-ˌtʃest | ɒn ə ˈlɑːdʒ ˈtʃaɪniːz ˈdʒʌŋk |

Joe plays Jazz
ˈdʒəʊ ˌpleɪz ˈdʒæz

Richard plays chess
ˈrɪtʃəd ˌpleɪz ˈtʃes

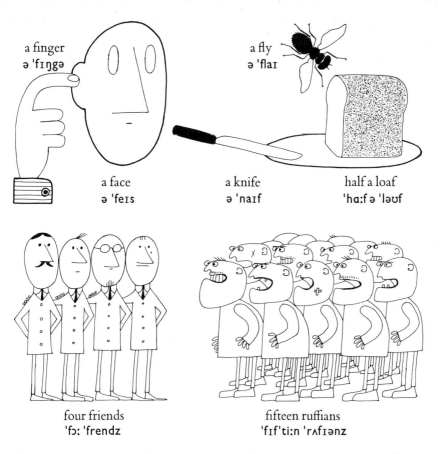

a finger
ə ˈfɪŋgə

a fly
ə ˈflaɪ

a face
ə ˈfeɪs

a knife
ə ˈnaɪf

half a loaf
ˈhɑːf ə ˈləʊf

four friends
ˈfɔː ˈfrendz

fifteen ruffians
ˈfɪfˈtiːn ˈrʌfɪənz

The rough, tough ruffians | make fierce faces | to frighten the four friends |
ðə ˈrʌf ˈtʌf ˈrʌfɪənz | meɪk ˈfɪəs ˈfeɪsɪz | tə ˈfraɪtn ðə ˈfɔː ˈfrendz |

The friends | fight off the ruffians |
ðə ˈfrendz | ˈfaɪt ˈɒf ðə ˈrʌfɪənz |
Four oafs | fall flat on the floor, | and the rest flee | in fear |
ˈfɔːr ˈəʊfs | ˈfɔːl ˈflæt | ɒn ðə ˈflɔː | ənd ðə ˈrest ˈfliː | ɪn ˈfɪə |

59

V

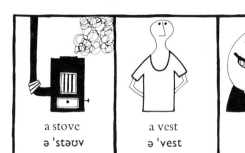

a stove	a vest	vice	virtue
ə ˈstəʊv	ə ˈvest	ˈvaɪs	ˈvɜːtjuː

seven evil devils
ˈsevn ˈiːvl ˈdevlz

a village vicar
ə ˈvɪlɪdʒ ˈvɪkə

Victor   Vivian   Eve   Vivienne
ˈvɪktə   ˈvɪviən   ˈiːv   ˈvɪviˈen

Every evening,
Victor and Vivian visit Eve |
ˈevrɪ ˈiːvnɪŋ |
ˈvɪktər ən ˈvɪviən ˈvɪzɪt ˈiːv |

Victor | and Vivian | are rivals
ˈvɪktər | ən ˈvɪviən | ə ˈraɪvlz |

Both vow | to love Eve | forever |
ˈbəʊθ ˈvaʊ | tə ˈlʌv ˈiːv | fəˈrevə |

But Eve is very vain. | Vivienne | is vivacious | and full of verve |
bət ˈiːv ɪz ˈverɪ ˈveɪn | vɪviˈen | ɪz vɪˈveɪʃəs | ən ˈfʊl əv ˈvɜːv |

Eventually, Victor gives Eve up |
and goes over to Vivienne, |
leaving Eve | to Vivian |
ɪˈventʃʊəlɪ ˈvɪktə gɪvz ˈiːv ˈʌp |
ən gəʊz ˈəʊvə tə vɪviˈen |
ˈliːvɪŋ ˈiːv | tə ˈvɪviən |

3   33   33,333

θ

3
'θriː

33
'θɜːtɪ 'θriː

33,333
'θɜːtɪ | 'θriː | 'θaʊznd |
'θriː | 'hʌndrəd | n 'θɜːtɪ | 'θriː

Arthur Smith, | a thick-set, healthy athlete | sees three thieves |
throw a thong | round Thea's throat | and threaten to throttle her |
'ɑːθə 'smɪθ | ə 'θɪkset 'helθɪ 'æθliːt | siːz 'θriː 'θiːvz |
'θrəʊ ə 'θɒŋ | raʊnd 'θɪəz 'θrəʊt | ən 'θretn tə 'θrɒtl ə |

FILTHY!

He throws one thug | to earth | with a thud | that shakes his teeth |
Both the other thieves run off | with a filthy oath |
hɪ 'θrəʊz 'wʌn 'θʌg | tʊ 'ɜːθ | wɪð ə θʌd | ðət 'ʃeɪks ɪz 'tiːθ |
'bəʊθ ðɪ 'ʌðə 'θiːvz 'rʌn 'ɒf | wɪð ə 'fɪlθɪ 'əʊθ |

Thea | thanks Arthur | for
thrashing the three thugs |
'θɪə 'θæŋks 'ɑːθə | fə
'θræʃɪŋ ðə 'θriː 'θʌgz |

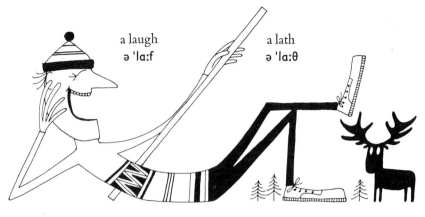

a laugh
ə ˈlɑːf

a lath
ə ˈlɑːθ

a thin Finn
ə ˈθɪn ˈfɪn

Frances has a First
ˈfrɑːnsɪs hæz ə ˈfɜːst

Francis has a thirst
ˈfrɑːnsɪs hæz ə ˈθɜːst

Philip fought |
while Philippa thought |
ˈfɪlɪp ˈfɔːt |
waɪl ˈfɪlɪpə ˈθɔːt |

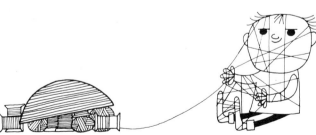

This useful thread is free
ˈðɪs ˈjuːsfl ˈθred ɪz ˈfriː

This youthful Fred is three
ˈðɪs ˈjuːθfl ˈfred ɪz ˈθriː

ð

weather
'weðə

wreaths
'ri:ðz

a feather
ə 'feðə

a leather tether
ə 'leðə 'teðə

These bathers | are breathing |
through their mouths |
'ðiːz 'beɪðəz | ə 'briːðɪŋ |
θruː ðɛə 'maʊðz |

Smooth breathing |
is rather soothing |
'smuːð 'briːðɪŋ |
ɪz 'raːðə 'suːðɪŋ |

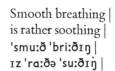

These are three brothers
'ðiːz ə 'θriː 'brʌðəz

This is their other brother
'ðɪs ɪz ðɛər 'ʌðə 'brʌðə

These are their
father and mother
'ðiːz ə ðɛə
'faːðər ən 'mʌðə

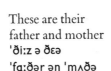

Their other brother is teething
ðɛər 'ʌðə 'brʌðər ɪz 'tiːðɪŋ

63

some spinsters
səm 'spɪnstəz

a saw
ə 'sɔː

several mice
'sevərəl 'maɪs

a saucer
ə 'sɔːsə

seven sausages
'sevn 'sɒsɪdʒɪz

Sue | and Cecily | are sisters |
'suː | ənd 'sɪsɪlɪ | ə 'sɪstəz |

Sue | is sixteen | this summer |
'suː | ɪz sɪk'stiːn | ðɪs 'sʌmə |

Cecily | was seventeen | last Sunday |
'sɪsɪlɪ | wəz 'sevntiːn | laːst 'sʌndɪ |

Sue | is sowing | grass | seed. | She sees Cecily | asleep |
with a glass | of cyder | and a nice sixpenny ice | by her side. |
Sue | slips across, | sips the glass | of cyder | and eats the ice |
'suː | ɪz 'səʊɪŋ | 'graːs | ,siːd | ʃɪ 'siːz 'sɪsɪlɪ | ə'sliːp |
wɪð ə 'glaːs | əv 'saɪdə | ənd ə 'sɪkspənɪ 'aɪs | baɪ ɜː ˌsaɪd |
'suː | 'slɪps ə'krɒs | 'sɪps ðə 'glaːs | əv 'saɪdə | ənd 'iːts ðɪ 'aɪs |

Cecily | gets such a surprise |
when she wakes |
ˌsɪsɪlɪ | gets 'sʌtʃ ə sə'praɪz |
wen ʃɪ 'weɪks |

64

a zoo
ə 'zuː

cages
'keɪdʒɪz

prison bars
'prɪzn 'bɑːz

a zebra
ə 'zebrə

a zebu
ə 'ziːbjuː

daisies
'deɪzɪz

Zoe is visiting the zoo
'zəʊɪ ɪz 'vɪzɪtɪŋ ðə 'zuː

A lazy zebra | called Desmond | is dozing | at the zoo |
He feels flies | buzzing | round his eyes, | ears and nose |
ə 'leɪzɪ 'zebrə | ˌkɔːld 'dezmənd | ɪz 'dəʊzɪŋ | ət ðə 'zuː |
hɪ 'fiːlz 'flaɪz | 'bʌzɪŋ | raʊnd ɪz 'aɪz | 'ɪəz ənd 'nəʊz |

He rouses, | opens his eyes, | rises and goes | to Zoe |
Zoe | is wearing a rose | on her blouse. | Zoe gives Desmond these buns |
hɪ 'raʊzɪz | 'əʊpənz ɪz 'aɪz | 'raɪzɪz ən 'gəʊz | tə 'zəʊɪ |
'zəʊɪ | ɪz 'weərɪŋ ə 'rəʊz | ɒn ɜː 'blaʊz | 'zəʊɪ 'gɪvz 'dezmənd 'ðiːz 'bʌnz |

Z

a thumb	a sum
ə ˈθʌm	ə ˈsʌm

a mouth	a mouse
ə ˈmaʊθ	ə ˈmaʊs

a path	a pass
ə ˈpɑːθ	ə ˈpɑːs

a race	a wraith
ə ˈreɪs	ə ˈreɪθ

The cook thickens the soup
ðə ˈkʊk ˈθɪkənz ðə ˈsuːp

The soup sickens the cook
ðə ˈsuːp ˈsɪkənz ðə ˈkʊk

This atheist has lost faith
ðɪs ˈeɪθɪɪst əz ˈlɒst ˈfeɪθ

This asiatic has lost face
ðɪs eɪʃɪˈætɪk əz ˈlɒst ˈfeɪs

⟨	MAY	⟩			
Su	*	5	12	19	26
M	*	6	13	20	27
T	*	7	14	21	28
W	1	8	15	22	29
Th	2	9	16	23	30
F	3	10	17	24	31
Sa	4	11	18	25	*

The third Thursday | of this month |
is the sixteenth |
ðə 'θɜːd 'θɜːzdɪ | əv 'ðɪs 'mʌnθ |
ɪz ðə 'sɪk'stiːnθ |

Mosquitoes are rising...
mɒsˈkiːtəʊz ə ˈraɪzɪŋ

The fishermen are writhing
ðə ˈfɪʃəmən ə ˈraɪðɪŋ

an endless fence |
across the endless fens |
ən ˈendlɪs ˈfens |
əˈkrɒs ðɪ ˈendlɪs ˈfenz |

a few pens | costing a few pence |
ə ˈfjuː ˈpenz | ˌkɒstɪŋ ə ˈfjuː ˈpens |

67

ʃ

sunshine
'sʌnʃaɪn

rubbish
'rʌbɪʃ

Sheila
'ʃiːlə

a rash
ə 'ræʃ

a shawl
ə 'ʃɔːl

a traditional politician
ə trə'dɪʃənl pɒlɪ'tɪʃn

This shop is a fish shop
'ðɪʃ 'ʃɒp ɪz ə 'fɪʃ ˌʃɒp

six sheep
'sɪkʃ 'ʃiːp

a mission station in the bush
ə 'mɪʃn ˌsteɪʃn ɪn ðə 'bʊʃ

Sheila | has just finished | washing | this sheet | in her washing-machine |
'ʃiːlə | həz 'dʒʌst 'fɪnɪʃt | 'wɒʃɪŋ | ðɪʃ 'ʃiːt | ɪn ɜː 'wɒʃɪŋ məˌʃiːn |

camouflage
'kæməflɑːʒ

invasion
ɪn'veɪʒn

a vision
ə 'vɪʒn

a tape measure
ə 'teɪp ˌmeʒə

treasure
'treʒə

rouge
'ruːʒ

The unusual confusion | surrounding the revision | of the decision |
regarding the seizure | and closure | of the garage |
is surely due | to some measure | of collusion |
ðɪ ʌn'juːʒwəl kən'fjuːʒn | səˌraʊndɪŋ ðə rɪ'vɪʒn | əv ðə dɪ'sɪʒn |
rɪˌgɑːdɪŋ ðə 'siːʒər | ənd 'kləʊʒər | əv ðə 'gærɑːʒ |
ɪʒ 'ʃʊəlɪ 'djuː | tə ˌsʌm 'meʒər | əv kə'luːʒn |

m

a comb
ə ˈkəʊm

the moon
ðə ˈmuːn

a maid
ə ˈmeɪd

a milkman
ə ˈmɪlkmən

a lamp
ə ˈlæmp

some mushrooms
səm ˈmʌʃruːmz

Marmaduke | and Mary | have mumps |
ˈmɑːmədjuːk | əm ˈmɛəri | hæv ˈmʌmps |

They mustn't munch | marmalade | sandwiches | at the moment, | says Mummy
ðeɪ ˈmʌsnt ˈmʌntʃ | ˈmɑːməleɪd | ˈsæmwɪdʒɪz | ət ðə ˈməʊmənt | sez ˈmʌmɪ |

An immense mammoth | in the museum | at Memphis |
ən ɪˈmens ˈmæməθ | ɪn ðə mjuːˈzɪəm | ət ˈmemfɪs |

The museum | has many memorable monuments | to the memory of
some remarkable members | of the Moslem community |
ðə mjuːˈzɪəm | hæz ˈmenɪ ˈmemərəbl ˈmɒnjuːmənts | tə ðə ˈmemərɪ əv
səm rɪˈmɑːkəbl ˈmembəz | əv ðə ˈmɒzləm kəˈmjuːnɪtɪ |

a bone	a tin can	a cannon	an urn
ə ˈbəʊn	ə ˈtɪn ˈkæn	ə ˈkænən	ən ˈɜːn

a thin man	nine nuns
ə ˈθɪn ˈmæn	ˈnaɪn ˈnʌnz

Naughty Nancy | has bent the knitting needles | and knotted Nanny's knitting |
ˈnɔːtɪ ˈnænsɪ | həz ˈbent ðə ˈnɪtɪŋ ˌniːdlz | ən ˈnɒtɪd ˈnænɪz ˈnɪtɪŋ |

Henry hands his nephew Nigel a brand-new pound-note | on Sundays |
ˈhenrɪ ˈhændz ɪz ˈnevjuː ˈnaɪdzl ə ˈbrænˈnjuː ˈpaʊndˈnəʊt | ɒn ˈsʌndɪz |

Norman Brown | signs | his name | again | and again | with a fine pen line |
ˈnɔːmən ˈbraʊn | ˈsaɪnz | ɪz ˈneɪm | əˈgen | ənd əˈgen | wɪð ə ˈfaɪn ˈpen ˌlaɪn |

71

ŋ

an anchor
ən 'æŋkə

a tankard
ə 'tæŋkəd

a monkey   string   a singer   a stronger singer
ə 'mʌŋkɪ   'strɪŋ   ə 'sɪŋə   ə 'strɒŋgə ˌsɪŋə

a strong young monk |
beating a hanging gong |
ə 'strɒŋ 'jʌŋ 'mʌŋk |
'biːtɪŋ ə 'hæŋɪŋ 'gɒŋ |

a ringed finger
ə 'rɪŋd 'fɪŋgə

English rankers | marching along | singing | a rousing drinking-song |
'ɪŋglɪʃ 'ræŋkəz | 'mɑːtʃɪŋ ə'lɒŋ | 'sɪŋɪŋ | ə 'raʊzɪŋ 'drɪŋkɪŋ-sɒŋ |

a pair of robins
ə ˈpeər əv ˈrɒbɪnz

a shipwrecked mariner
ə ˈʃɪpˌrekt ˈmærɪnə

a wreck
ə ˈrek

a tree-trunk
ə ˈtriː ˌtrʌŋk

a rope
ə ˈrəup

rocks
ˈrɒks

a rubber ring
ə ˈrʌbə ˈrɪŋ

This rusty wreck | has run aground | on the rocks | of the Barrier Reef |
ðɪs ˈrʌstɪ ˈrek | əz ˈrʌn əˈgraund | ɒn ðə ˈrɒks | əv ðə ˈbærɪə ˈriːf |

Rowena | is very rich | and rides | her mare | in Rotten Row |
rəʊˈiːnə | ɪz ˈverɪ ˈrɪtʃ | ənd ˈraɪdz | ɜː ˈmeər | ɪn ˈrɒtn ˈrəʊ |

Strawberries, | raspberries and red-currants |
with real cream | are really very refreshing |
'strɔːbrɪz | 'rɑːzbrɪz ənd 'red'kʌrənts |
wɪð 'rɪəl 'kriːm | ə ˌrɪəlɪ 'verɪ rɪ'freʃɪŋ |

This train | and its trucks | are trapped | by a tree-trunk | across the track |
'ðɪs 'treɪn | ənd ɪts 'trʌks | ə 'træpt | baɪ ə 'triːˌtrʌŋk | ə'krɒs ðə 'træk |

Three hundred readers | used the library | reading room |
in the period | from February to April, | reports the librarian
'θriː 'hʌndrəd 'riːdəz | 'juːzd ðə 'laɪbrarɪ | 'riːdɪŋ ˌruːm |
ɪn ðə 'pɪərɪəd | frəm 'februərɪ tʊ 'eɪprəl | rɪ ˌpɔːts ðə laɪˌbrɛərɪən |

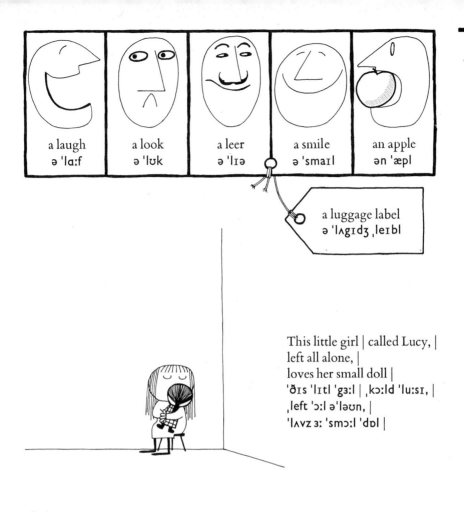

a laugh ə 'lɑːf	a look ə 'lʊk	a leer ə 'lɪə	a smile ə 'smaɪl	an apple ən 'æpl

a luggage label
ə 'lʌgɪdʒ ˌleɪbl

This little girl | called Lucy, |
left all alone, |
loves her small doll |
'ðɪs 'lɪtl 'gɜːl, ˌkɔːld 'luːsɪ, |
ˌleft 'ɔːl ə'ləʊn, |
'lʌvz ɜː 'smɔːl 'dɒl |

a lark
ə 'lɑːk

A noble old lion | and lioness | lying asleep | in their lair |
ə 'nəʊbl əʊld 'laɪən | ənd 'laɪə'nes | 'laɪɪŋ ə'sliːp | ɪn ðeə 'leə |

a small pool | lying on a low hill | on a large island | in a lovely lake |
in the Welsh hills |
ə 'smɔːl 'puːl | ˌlaɪɪŋ ɒn ə 'ləʊ 'hɪl | ɒn ə 'lɑːdʒ 'aɪlənd | ɪn ə 'lʌvlɪ 'leɪk |
ɪn ðə 'welʃ 'hɪlz |

Eleven local lads | and lasses | dancing | round
the village | maypole | to a tuneful old melody |
ɪ'levn 'ləʊkl 'lædz | n 'læsɪz | 'dɑːnsɪŋ | raʊnd
ðə 'vɪlɪdʒ | 'meɪpəʊl | tʊ ə 'tjuːnfl əʊld 'melədɪ |

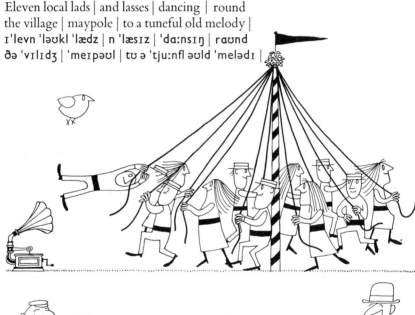

The tall pole topples | and falls, | but all the people laugh |
and the lads and girls are still able to smile |
ðə 'tɔːl 'pəʊl 'tɒplz | ənd 'fɔːlz | bət 'ɔːl ðə 'piːpl 'lɑːf |
ən ðə 'lædz ən 'gɜːlz ə 'stɪl 'eɪbl tə 'smaɪl |

| a haddock ə ˈhædɒk | a hare ə ˈhɛə | a hawk ə ˈhɔːk | a hyena ə haɪˈiːnə |
| a heron ə ˈherən | a hippopotamus ə hɪpəˈpɒtəməs | a herring ə ˈherɪŋ | a hedgehog ə ˈhedʒhɒg |

Humble, hairy Herbert |
has his hand on his heart |
ˈhʌmbl ˈhɛəri ˈhɜːbət |
hæz ɪz ˈhænd ɒn ɪz ˈhɑːt |

Henry's horse | has hurt his hoof | in a hole | while hunting |
Henry helps him | to hobble home |
ˈhenrɪz ˈhɔːs | əz ˈhɜːt ɪz ˈhuːf | ɪn ə ˈhəʊl | waɪl ˈhʌntɪŋ |
ˈhenrɪ ˈhelps ɪm | tə ˈhɒbl ˈhəʊm |

Ellen
'elən

Helen
'helən

Ellen is hearty
'elən ɪz 'hɑːtɪ

Helen is arty
'helən ɪz 'ɑːtɪ

Ellen heats up the pie
'elən 'hiːts ʌp ðə 'paɪ

Helen eats up the pie
'helən 'iːts ʌp ðə 'paɪ

Ellen looks after her heir
'elən lʊks 'ɑːftə hɜːr 'ɛə

Helen looks after her hair
'helən lʊks 'ɑːftər ɜː 'hɛə

Ellen and Hannah like harbours
'elən ənd 'hænə laɪk 'hɑːbəz

Helen and Anna like arbours
'helən ənd 'ænə laɪk 'ɑːbəz

a cube
ə 'kju:b

a new suit
ə 'nju: 'sju:t

a stupid youth
ə 'stju:pɪd 'ju:θ

a newt
ə 'nju:t

a curious curate
ə 'kjʊərɪəs 'kjʊərət

a young yak
ə 'jʌŋ 'jæk

a yelping yapping terrier
ə 'jelpɪŋ 'jæpɪŋ 'terɪə

Young Una | is beautiful | and alluring |
in her superb new yellow tunic |
'jʌŋ 'ju:nə | ɪz 'bju:tɪfl | ənd ə'ljʊərɪŋ |
ɪn ɜ: sju:'pɜ:b ˌnju: 'jeləʊ 'tju:nɪk |

Una's tutor | Hugo | is an amusing
humorous musician |
'ju:nəz 'tju:tə | 'hju:gəʊ | ɪz ən
ə'mju:zɪŋ 'hju:mərəs mju:'zɪʃn |

Hugo's tuneful duet | for tuba | and euphonium | is musically unique |
'hju:gəʊz 'tju:nfl dju:'et | fə 'tju:bə | ənd ju:'fəʊnɪəm | ɪz 'mju:zɪ'kəlɪ ju:'ni:k |

j

79

w

a window
ə ˈwɪndəʊ

the Wild West
ðə ˈwaɪld ˈwest

a weeping willow
ə ˈwiːpɪŋ ˈwɪləʊ

a wicked woman
ə ˈwɪkɪd ˈwʊmən

a sweet white wine
ə ˈswiːt ˈwaɪt ˈwaɪn

a wig
ə ˈwɪg

William | is worried | about woodworm | in the woodwork | of his wardrobe |
ˈwɪljəm | ɪz ˈwʌrɪd | əbaʊt ˈwʊdwɜːm | ɪn ðə ˈwʊdwɜːk | əv ɪz ˈwɔːdrəʊb |

Why wouldn't Walter wash | with water | that wasn't warm? | Walter works | at a waxworks | and wax won't wash off | without warm water |
ˈwaɪ ˈwʊdnt ˈwɔːltə ˈwɒʃ | wɪð ˈwɔːtə | ðət ˈwɒznt ˈwɔːm | ˈwɔːltə ˈwɜːks | ət ə ˈwæksˌwɜːks | ənd ˈwæks ˈwəʊnt ˈwɒʃ ˈɒf | wɪˈðaʊt ˈwɔːm ˈwɔːtə |

a vale	a whale	a viper	a wiper
ə 'veɪl	ə 'weɪl	ə 'vaɪpə	ə 'waɪpə

a verse
ə 'vɜːs

a worse verse
ə 'wɜːs 'vɜːs

Why is the worse verse
worse than the first verse?
'waɪ ɪz ðə 'wɜːs 'vɜːs
'wɜːs ðən ðə 'fɜːst ˌvɜːs

William always wears a very
warm woollen vest | in winter |
'wɪljəm 'ɔːlwəz 'wɛəz ə 'verɪ
'wɔːm 'wʊlən 'vest | ɪn 'wɪntə |

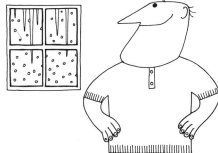

Victor, however, will never
wear woollen underwear, |
even in the Wild West |
'vɪktə haʊ'evə wɪl 'nevə
ˌwɛə 'wʊlən 'ʌndəwɛə |
'iːvn ɪn ðə 'waɪld 'west |

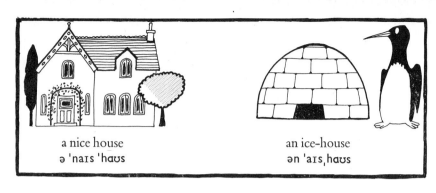

a nice house
ə ˈnaɪs ˈhaʊs

an ice-house
ən ˈaɪsˌhaʊs

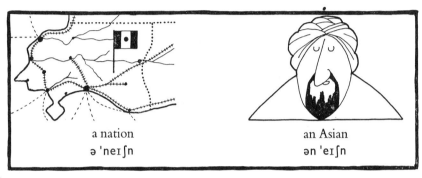

a nation
ə ˈneɪʃn̩

an Asian
ən ˈeɪʃn̩

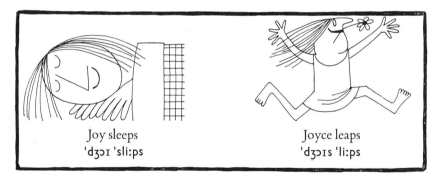

Joy sleeps
ˈdʒɔɪ ˈsliːps

Joyce leaps
ˈdʒɔɪs ˈliːps

a grey tabby
ə ˈɡreɪ ˈtæbɪ

a great abbey
ə ˈɡreɪt ˈæbɪ

a Greek spy
ə ˈgriːk ˈspaɪ

a Greek's pie
ə ˈgriːks ˈpaɪ

John said that all men could come
ˈdʒɒn sed ðət ˈɔːl men kəd ˌkʌm

Joan said the tall men could come
ˈdʒoʊn sed ðə ˈtɔːl men kəd ˈkʌm

I scream
aɪ ˈskriːm

Ice cream
ˌaɪs ˈkriːm

I saw her race
aɪ ˈsɔː hɜː ˈreɪs

I saw her ace
aɪ ˈsɔː hɜːr ˈeɪs

Word indexes

These indexes contain the words used in the book, either in the inflected form in which they actually occur, or in their simple uninflected form. They provide teachers and students with classified word material, which can be used for further practice or systematic revision. Page references are not given, but the indexes are presented both in a normal and a reverse form. In both cases the order of phonemes in the word serves as a basis rather than the order of letters. The 'alphabetic order' is then provided by the order in which the phonemes are introduced in the book (see the table of contents, pp. 5–6).

The forward index groups together words which alliterate but contrast in the final segment. The reverse index brings together those which rhyme, but contrast in the initial segment. By reference first to the forward index, then to the reverse index, all words in the book exemplifying a given phoneme in initial and final position are immediately available. (The underlined words have been recorded on the tape.)

Forward index

This index groups words according to their initial phonemes. It provides alliterative sets and contrasting sets of vowels and final consonants.

iː eat, Eve, even, evening, evil, easy.

ɪ it, expensive, expansive, exam, examine, itch, itching, eventually, is, immense, in, enjoy, invasion, English, eleven.

e egg, ever, every, enter, end, endless, Ellen.

æ apple, abbey, abacus, at, adder, avid, athlete, ass, amateur, Anne, Anna, and, Anderson, anchor.

ʌ other, underwear, unusual, uncouth.

ɑː are, arbour, art, arty, arch, after, Arthur, arm.

ɒ off, of, on, orange, Olive.

ɔː or, all, alderman, Aldeburgh.

uː ooh!

ɜː er..., urge, earth, earthworm, urn, earl.

ə apart, apartment, observe, adoring, adventurous, adroit, again, aground, astronomer, astrologer, asleep, amid, amusing, annoying, arrive, alone, alluring.

eɪ able, eight, age, aged, atheist, ace, Asian.

aɪ I, eye, ice, eyes, island.

ɔɪ oyster.

əʊ oh!, open, ogre, oaf, over, overcoat, overgrown, oath, old.

aʊ our, out, outboard, owl.

ɪə ear.

ɛə heir.

84

p   peep, people, piece, pip, picnic, pig, <u>pimple</u>, pin, pet, pedal, pen, penny, pence, pens, pat, Pat, paddle, pack, passenger, <u>puppy</u>, public, puck, puff, park, path, pass, passport, palm, poppy, pot, Polly, politician, paw, portrait, pork, Paul, put, putting, pudding, pull, pulling, pool, purposeful, Perkins, purse, pearl, potato, policeman, politely, <u>paper</u>, pain, pipe, pies, pine, pint, poise, point, poach, poacher, pole, pound, peer, period, pair, poor, <u>pre-packed</u>, pretty, prison, prosperous, professor, professional, pray, proud, plait, play, plate, played, plane, plough, piano.

b   bee, beat, beach, beast, bean, because, big, biscuit, bin, Bessie, bent, bat, batter, battle, battler, back, band, bang, bank, banker, barrier, <u>bubble</u>, but, butter, butler, buddy, buck, buxom, bug, buzz, bun, bunker, bar, Barbara, bard, bark, bath, bars, barmaid, barn, bobby, bottom, bottle, body, bog, bomb, bought, ball, book, bookish, butcher, bush, bull, boot, bird, burglar, birth, birthday, baboon, banana, balloon, baby, bait, bake, bathe, bather, by, <u>bible</u>, bite, bicycle, boy, bow (əʊ), boat, both, bone, bold, bow (aʊ), bower, bounce, beer, bear, boor, breathe, bring, breath, brand, brother, brute, <u>bray</u>, break, bright, brown, blissful, black, blot, block, blonde, <u>blue</u>, blew, blouse, beautiful.

t   tea, tin, Ted, tether, tempt, ten, tent, terrier, terrible, tabby, tank, tankard, tough, tart, top, topple, <u>tot</u>, totter, talk, tall, took, too, two, tooth, turtle, tape, take, <u>tie</u>, tyre, tired, time, toy, toil, toe, toad, toadstool, toast, tower, towel, town, tier, tear (ɪə), tear (ɛə), tour, tourist, <u>tree</u>, tree-trunk, trick, trill, treasure, treasury, trap, track, tramp, truck, tradition, tray, train, try, trousers, tuba, tutor, tunic, tuneful, twins, <u>twelve</u>.

d   deep, decline, devout, decision, decide, despair, distant, destroy, dish, dead, devil, desert, Desmond, Dad, Daddy, dank, duck, dust, dusty, does, doesn't, dun, Dundas, dungeon, dark, darn, dance, darling, dock, docker, docks, dog, don, doll, daughter, dawn, <u>do</u>, doom, dirt, dirty, day, daybreak, David, daisy, die, dine, Dinah, dodo, doze, dowdy, down, deer, dear, dearly, Deirdre, dairy, dour, dream, drink, drill, dread, dreadful, <u>drug</u>, dromedary, drown, drear, dreary, <u>due</u>, duet, duel, duke.

k   kitten, <u>kick</u>, kitchen, kiss, king, Ken, cap, <u>cat</u>, cactus, catch, camouflage, camera, can, cannon, cup, Cuthbert, custard, cousin, come, comfort, comfortable, country, constable, carp, carpet, cart, calf, castle, can't, cock, coffee, cosset, cost, cork, corset, cormorant, corner, call, called, cook, cookery, curl, curly, community, confusion, conspire, collusion, Kate, cake, cage, kite, coy, quoit, coat, coast, coastal, comb, cone, coal, cold, cow, coward, cowed, cowl, cowled, care, courier, cream, crusty, crumpet, crock, crockery, cross, crawl, <u>cry</u>, crone, crowd, crown, cruel, clap, climb, closed, closure, <u>clear</u>, cure, curious, curate, cube, <u>quick</u>, quickly, quite.

g   <u>giggle</u>, get, guest, garage, government, gusto, gun, guard, garden, guardsman, <u>gargle</u>, gargoyle, gong, gorse, good, goose, ghoul, girl, gate, gave, gaze, guide, <u>go</u>, goat, goal, gold, golden, greedy, Greek, grand, grass, grey, great, <u>grow</u>, grown, grouse, ground, glove, glum, glass, glower, glare.

tʃ   cheap, cheese, chips, chicken, chin, chill, check, Czech, chess, chest, chubby, chuckle, chance, Charles, chop, chew, choose, church, chase, chain, Chinese, child, choice, cheer, cheerful, chair.

dʒ   Jean, gin, Jill, Jeremy, Jen, generous, jelly, jacket, jazz, jam-jar, jug, judge, just, jump, jar, John, jolly, juicy, jerk, jersey, James, Jane, Giles, Joy, Joyce, Joe, Joan, Jones, jeer, jury.

f   feet, feel, fit, figure, fifteen, fish, Finn, finish, finger, Philip, Philippa, filth, filthy, February, feather, fen, fence, fens, fell, fat, fact, fashion, fashionable, father, farm, farmer, farmyard, fog, for, four, fought, faun, fall, full, food, fool, foolish, fur, first, fern, photographer, forever, faith, face, fail, fire, fight, five, fine, find, file, foil, photograph, focus, phone, foal, fountain, found, fowl, fear, fierce, fair, fairy, fair-haired, Freda, Fred, friend, Francis, Frances, from, fright, frighten, frightful, frightfully, flee, fleet, flat, flag, floor, flirt, fly, flight, float, flower, flowery, few, furious, fuel.

v   vicar, Vivienne, vivacious, visit, visitor, vision, village, vest, virtue, verve, verse, vain, vale, viper, vice, vow, vary, various.

θ   thief, thieves, thick, thicken, thick-set, thin, thing, thank, thanks, thud, thug, thumb, thump, thong, thought, thirty, third, thirst, Thursday, Thea, theatre, three, threat, threaten, thread, thrash, throttle, through, throw.

ð   these, this, that, the, they, though, there, their.

s   see, sea, seed, seek, seizure, sip, sick, sicken, six, sixpenny, sixteen, sixteenth, Cecily, sister, sing, singer, sink, seven, seventeen, several, says, sell, seller, sandwich, supper, suburb, suck, such, sum, some, summer, summon, sun, son, Sunday, sock, sausage, song, saw, saucer, Sue, soup, soothe, Sir, serpent, circus, circle, surprise, surround, say, sail, sailor, side, cyder, size, sign, soil, so, sow, soap, sour, sound, seer, Sarah, spin, spinster, spot, sport, space, spy, spire, spoil, spear, spare, Stephen, still, stamp, stand, stump, stalk, stalker, storm, stormy, stool, stile, stoke, stoker, stone, stare, string, strong, straw, strawberry, stranger, stroll, stupid, school, skirt, sky, scout, scowl, scare, scream, scratch, squat, squirm, Smith, small, smooth, smile, snatch, sneer, slip, slipper, slack, slow, superb, suit, sweet, swear.

z   zebu, zebra, zoo, Zoe, zoologist.

ʃ   she, sheep, sheet, Sheila, ship, ship-wrecked, shatter, shutter, shark, shop, shopper, shock, short, shawl, sugar, shoe, shoot, shake, shy, show, shower, shout, share, sure, surely.

m   meal, Mr, mission, mill, milk, milkman, measure, memory, memorable, member, Memphis, men, many, melody, map, mash, mammoth, man, mariner, mother, mustard, mush, mushroom, Mummy, mumps, munch, monk, monkey, Mark, march, mast, Marmaduke, marmalade, mosquito, Moslem, monument, Maud, move, moose, moon, may, mate, maid, make, mice, motor, motor-boat, moment, mouth (θ), mouth (ð), mouse, mountain, mound, mare, Mary, museum, music, musical, musician, mural.

n   needle, knit, net, never, nephew, nest, gnat, nanny, Nancy, nun, not, knot, knotted, naughty, Norman, nation, name, night, Nigel, knife, nice, noise, noisy, <u>no</u>, noble, note, nose, near, nearly, <u>new</u>, newt.

r   read, reader, reach, reef, wreath, report, retort, rich, Richard, refreshing, revision, remarkable, ring, ringed, red, red-currant, wreck, rest, wren, rat, rash, rank, ranker, rubber, <u>rough</u>, rust, rusty, run, runner, rajah, rather, raspberry, robin, <u>rot</u>, rotten, rock, Roger, rook, rude, rouge, room, rule, ruler, wraith, race, rain, rainy, rail, railway, ride, rival, writhe, rise, <u>Roy</u>, royal, row(əʊ), Rowena, rope, robe, rose, Rome, roll, roller, <u>row</u> (aʊ), rout, rouse, round, rear, real, really, <u>rare</u>.

l   leap, lead, leaf, leave, little, lid, list, letter, leg, <u>left</u>, leather, lad, ladder, lass, lamp, luggage, love, lover, <u>lovely</u>, lunch, lark, large, laugh, larva, lath, last, lot, lock, log, lost, lord, <u>lawn</u>, look, loose, Lucy, lose, lurk, <u>lay</u>, label, lake, lazy, lie, liar, lion, lioness, <u>library</u>, like, line, loyal, low, load, local, loaf, lout, loud, Lear, leer, lair, <u>lure</u>, lurid.

h   he, heat, hippopotamus, hill, <u>head</u>, hedgehog, hen, Henry, herring, heron, Helen, help, held, <u>health</u>, healthy, hat, had, haddock, hack, hacking, Hanna, hand, hang, <u>Harry</u>, hut, hug, humble, hunt, hundred, harp, harbour, heart, hearty, hard, half, hot, hog, hawk, horse, hoop, hoof, <u>her</u>, Herbert, hurt, hate, high, hyena, higher, height, Hoyle, hope, home, <u>hole</u>, how, however, Howard, house, hound, howl, <u>here</u>, hero, hair, hairy, Hugo, huge, <u>humour</u>.

j   <u>yellow</u>, yelp, yap, yak, <u>young</u>, yard, yacht, <u>yawn</u>, <u>you</u>, euphonium, youth, youthful, use(s), useful, use(z), unique, <u>Una</u>.

w   we, weep, wicked, which, witch, with, without, whistle, women, winter, window, <u>will</u>, willow, William, wed, wedding-dress, weather, west, well, well-dressed, Welsh, wax, wax-works, <u>one</u>, wonder, worry, worried, watch, watch-chain, was, wash, washing-machine, water, wardrobe, walk, warm, warn, wall, Walter, would, wood, woodwork, woodworm, woman, wool, woollen, were, work, worse, worm, way, wait, wake, wave, whale, <u>why</u>, wire, wipe, wiper, white, whiting, wide, wine, wild, won't, weary, <u>wear</u>, wary, warily.

Reverse word index

This index orders words according to the last phonemes in the word.

iː   tee, tea, see, sea, <u>tree</u>, <u>free</u>, <u>three</u>, we.

ɪ   Zoe, sleepy, puppy, poppy, community, <u>pretty</u>, arty, hearty, naughty, beauty, dirty, thirty, dusty, rusty, crusty, monkey, abbey, tabby, chubby, bobby, baby, greedy, Daddy, buddy, body, melody, dowdy, Thursday, Sunday, zoology, coffee, healthy, <u>filthy</u>, Bessie, juicy, Lucy, Nancy, easy, jersey, daisy, lazy, noisy, Nanny, <u>Mummy</u>, stormy, Jeremy, penny, many, sixpenny, rainy, very, Harry, worry, crockery, cookery, treasury, memory, library, dreary, weary, dairy, fairy, Mary, hairy, wary, jury, February, flowery, country, strawberry, raspberry, dromedary, Deirdre, every, Henry,

Cecily, warily, jelly, Polly, folly, curly, frightfully, blissfully, dearly, nearly, really, sourly, surely, eventually, politely, musically, quickly, lovely.

ɑː   are, car, bar, jar.

ɔː   or, paw, adore, for, four, saw, straw, floor.

uː   ooh!, too, two, chew, Sue, shoe, zoo, through, blue, blew, you, virtue, Zebu, due, few, nephew, new, Hugh.

ɜː   er..., fur, sir, her, were.

ə   Philippa, slipper, supper, shopper, paper, viper, wiper, prosper, visitor, letter, tatter, batter, shatter, butter, shutter, totter, daughter, water, tutor, amateur, motor, theatre, after, sister, Mr, oyster, spinster, Walter, winter, enter, vicar, docker, stalker, stoker, anchor, banker, ranker, bunker, arbour, harbour, rubber, tuba, member, render, Freda, adder, ladder, cyder, wander, figure, sugar, ogre, finger, stronger, butcher, poacher, adventure, rajah, Roger, astrologer, ginger, passenger, photographer, ever, however, forever, never, larva, lover, over, Arthur, the, tether, feather, leather, weather, other, mother, brother, father, rather, bather, professor, saucer, seizure, measure, treasure, closure, summer, farmer, humour, astronomer, hyena, Rowena, mariner, examiner, Anna, Hannah, runner, banana, corner, Una, Dinah, singer, Barbara, Aldeburgh, camera, Sarah, zebra, Sheila, seller, sailor, ruler, roller, battler, butter, burglar.

eɪ   day, birthday, pray, bray, tray, grey, lay, play, railway.

aɪ   eye, pie, spy, by, goodbye, tie, die, sky, shy, try, cry, lie, fly, high, why.

ɔɪ   Roy, toy, coy, enjoy, annoy, destroy.

əʊ   oh, bow, toe, mosquito, potato, gusto, dodo, window, go, Hugo, Joe, though, so, sow, no, piano, row, hero, grow, throw, low, willow, yellow, show.

ɑʊ   bow, cow, vow, plough.

aɪə   spire, conspire, tyre, fire, liar, higher, wire.

ɑʊə   our, bower, tower, sour, shower, glower, flower.

ɪə   ear, peer, spear, beer, tear, tier, dear, deer, cheer, jeer, fear, Thea, seer, near, sneer, rear, terrier, barrier, courier, drear, Lear, leer, clear, here.

ɛə   heir, pair, spare, despair, bear, tear, stare, care, scare, chair, fair, there, their, share, mare, lair, glare, rare, hair, hare, wear, underwear, swear.

ʊə   poor, spoor, boor, tour, dour, skua, sure, cure, lure, allure.

p   peep, deep, cheap, sheep, leap, asleep, weep, pip, chip, sip, ship, Philip, ship, mop, clap, trap, yap, up, cup, carp, harp, top, chop, shop, soup, hope, tape, soap, rope, hope, pipe, stamp, lamp, tramp, stump, jump, thump, plump, help, yelp.

b   cube, superb, suburb, wardrobe.

t   eat, beat, feet, sheet, fleet, athlete, heat, sweet, it, carpet, crumpet, jacket, biscuit, fit, cosset, corset, visit, knit, curate, circlet, duet, pet, thick-set, net, threat, at, Pat, pat, cat, fat, that, gnat, plait, flat, rat, hat, but, hut, art, apart, tart, cart, heart, pot, spot, tot, not, knot, rot, lot, blot, hot, yacht, squat, report, passport, sport, bought, retort, fought, thought, short, put, foot, hoot, shoot, brute, suit, newt, skirt, dirt, flirt, hurt, Herbert, Cuthbert, comfort, desert, eight, bait, Kate, gate, mate, portrait, great, plate, wait, bite, kite, fight, invite, night, bright, fright, polite, quite, quoit, adroit, motor-boat, coat, overcoat, goat, note, float, out, scout, devout, without, shout, rout, lout, trapped, tempt, ship-wrecked, pre-packed, locked, baked, poached, left, beast, atheist, zoologist, tourist, list, guest, chest, vest, nest, rest, well-dressed, west, dust, just, rust, fast, mast, last, cost, lost, first, thirst, focussed, toast, coast, finished, mashed, mushed, tent, hunt, can't, serpent, distant, observant, monument, moment, apartment, government, red-currant, cormorant, pint, point, won't, doesn't.

d   seed, read, lead, stupid, knotted, wicked, aged, David, amid, avid, worried, lurid, lid, Ted, dead, red, gingerbread, dread, Fred, thread, head, wed, Dad, Lad, lad, thud, bard, guard, regard, hard, yard, farmyard, outboard, Maud, lord, good, wood, would, food, rude, bird, third, tattered, shattered, buttered, shuttered, custard, mustard, entered, tankard, Richard, hundred, Edward, maid, barmaid, guide, side, decide, ride, wide, toad, load, cowed, proud, crowd, loud, period, scared, fair-haired, tired, coward, Howard, closed, used, doomed, end, friend, stand, band, brand, grand, hand, hand-in-hand, blonde, summoned, Desmond, island, find, pound, found, sound, mound, round, surround, ground, aground, hound, ringed, felled, held, called, failed, child, wild, old, hold, cold, gold, cowled.

k   seek, unique, Greek, kick, chick, thick, sick, music, tunic, picnic, trick, public, quick, check, Czech, wreck, ship-wreck, pack, back, Jack, track, black, slack, hack, yak, puck, buck, duck, suck, truck, park, bark, dark, shark, Mark, lark, dock, cock, sock, shock, lock, block, rock, crock, pork, talk, stalk, cork, hawk, walk, book, cookery-book, took, cook, rook, look, duke, Marmaduke, Luke, jerk, lurk, work, woodwork, haddock, bake, take, cake, shake, make, break, daybreak, lake, wake, like, stoke, joke, ink, sink, drink, bank, tank, dank, thank, junk, monk, tree-trunk, milk.

g   pig, big, wig, egg, leg, flag, bug, jug, thug, drug, hug, bog, dog, fog, log, hog, hedgehog.

tʃ   beach, reach, itch, rich, witch, which, catch, snatch, scratch, such, arch, march, watch, church, poach, munch, lunch.

dʒ   luggage, sausage, sandwich, village, hedge, judge, large, barge, urge, age, cage, orange.

f   thief, reef, leaf, photograph, puff, tough, rough, calf, laugh, half, off, hoof, knife, oaf, loaf.

v   Eve, leave, expansive, expensive, give, Olive, love, glove, of, move, verve, observe, gave, wave, five, arrive, Clive, stove, twelve.

θ   teeth, wreath, Smith, breath, path, bath, lath, tooth, uncouth, youth, earth, birth, mammoth, wraith, faith, oath, both, mouth, sixteenth, month, filth, health.

ð   teethe, breathe, with, soothe, smooth, bathe, writhe.

s   piece, police, kiss, Memphis, this, Francis, Frances, bliss, endless, chess, lioness, wedding-dress, ass, lass, pass, glass, grass, cross, across, gorse, horse, use, goose, juice, moose, loose, purse, verse, worse, purpose, cactus, Dundas, circus, abacus, focus, vivacious, hippopotamus, prosperous, adventurous, generous, ace, space, chase, face, race, ice, vice, mice, nice, choice, Joyce, mouse, grouse, house, fierce, various, curious, furious, peeps, leaps, chips, sips, ships, slips, mumps, helps, eats, meets, heats, pets, gets, plaits, tarts, knots, reports, retorts, puts, boots, shoots, Cuthbert's, baits, bites, boats, shouts, louts, beasts, tourists, guests, monuments, seeks, kicks, six, Jack's, wax, trucks, strong-box, docks, rocks, looks, waxworks, bakes, takes, cakes, shakes, wakes, likes, thanks, oafs, pence, fence, immense, dance, chance, bounce.

z   cheese, these, sees, Chinese, trees, is, reaches, catches, watches, sausages, sandwiches, urges, cages, pieces, kisses, asses, lasses, chases, faces, Joyce's, Franz's, loses, daisies, gazes, rises, rouses, Charles's, dishes, fairies, strawberri raspberries, says, Jazz, has, buzz, bars, because, was, choose, shoes, lose, use, amuse, slippers, members, sisters, spinsters, wonders, rankers, mother's, bathers, trousers, gaze, plays, always, eyes, pies, size, rise, surprise, tries, crie flies, poise, boys, toys, enjoys, noise, destroys, toes, mosquitoes, potatoes, doze, windows, Hugo's, shows, nose, rose, vows, rouse, blouse, ears, cheers sneers, pairs, stares, wears, cures, spires, cowers, lads, decides, rides, friends, hands, eggs, hugs, thugs, bogs, dog's, thieves, leaves, loves, arrives, wreaths, mouths, feels, hills, Charles, calls, falls, pearls, curls, gargles, devils, rivals, coils, coals, dreams, screams, James, chinks, robins, Perkins, twins, pens, fens, hens, buns, nuns, ferns, opens, fountains, mountains, thickens, sickens, Jane's, planes, declines, Jones, ruffians, things.

ʃ   dish, fish, rubbish, bookish, finish, foolish, English, mash, rash, thrash, mush wash, bush, Welsh.

ʒ   garage, camouflage, rouge.

m   dream, cream, scream, jam, exam, come, thumb, sum, some, glum, arm, palm, farm, bomb, from, storm, warm, doom, room, mushroom, woodworm, earthworm, squirm, museum, euphonium, bottom, buxom, Moslem, William, name, time, climb, comb, Rome, home.

n   bean, fifteen, sixteen, seventeen, Jean, washing-machine, in, pin, spin, bin, robin, tin, chicken, chin, kitchen, gin, Finn, thin, women, examine, twin, Vivienne, pen, ten, Ken, again, Jen, fen, men, wren, hen, Anne, can, man, bun, dun, gun, son, sun, nun, run, one, barn, darn, on, don, John, dawn, faun, lawn, yawn, baboon, moon, balloon, urn, fern, open, kitten, threaten, rotten, frighten, fountain, mountain, garden, golden, thicken, sicken, dungeon, even, Stephen, seven, eleven, govern, Anderson, prison, cousin, politician, tradition, musician, mission, profession, fashion, asian, nation, vision, revision, decision, confusion, collusion, invasion, summon, Norman, woman, alderman, milkman, policeman, guardsman, cannon, heron, Ellen, Helen, woollen.

ŋ   fleeing, praying, braying, playing, lying, flying, annoying, sowing, weeping clapping, yapping, yelping, heating, visiting, knitting, squatting, flirting, waiting, whiting, floating, costing, hunting, reading, wedding, guarding, regarding, pudding, standing, surrounding, king, backing, bucking, barking blocking, walking, lurking, drinking, itching, scratching, marching, watching, leaving, thing, teething, breathing, soothing, bathing, writhing, dancing, bouncing, buzzing, choosing, amusing, rising, dozing, rousing, refreshing, thrashing, washing, dreaming, banging, hanging, squirming, combing, evening, singing, bringing, ring, herring, adoring, tottering, glaring, wearing, alluring, bring, string, darling, crawling, pulling, pedalling, paddling, giggling, bang, hang, gong, thong, song, strong, along, young.

l feel, meal, still, chill, Jill, mill, April, trill, drill, bill, will, fell, sell, well, doll, all, Paul, ball, tall, call, fall, shawl, small, crawl, wall, pull, bull, full, wool, pool, stool, toadstool, school, ghoul, fool, rule, earl, pearl, curl, girl, people, apple, topple, pimple, terrible, bubble, hobble, comfortable, constable, remarkable, fashionable, memorable, able, label, bible, noble, humble, little, battle, bottle, throttle, turtle, Myrtle, coastal, needle, pedal, paddle, bicycle, musical, chuckle, circle, local, giggle, gargle, Nigel, beautiful, cheerful, frightful, dreadful, youthful, blissful, useful, purposeful, tuneful, evil, devil, rival, whistle, castle, official, traditional, professional, mural, several, unusual, fail, vale, sail, rail, whale, stile, file, smile, spoil, toil, gargoyle, foil, soil, royal, loyal, Hoyle, pole, maypole, coal, goal, foal, roll, stroll, hole, owl, towel, cowl, scowl, fowl, howl, real, duel, fuel, cruel.

Minimal pairs

In view of the special importance given to 'minimal pairs' in this book a comprehensive list is given below, classified according to the order of the respective phonemes. The word pairs may then be used by teachers (and self-instructional students working with informants or recordings) in the ways suggested in the instructions for use (pp. 9–13).

iː/ɪ	eat, it; ease, is; peep, pip; bean, bin; bargees, barges; cheap, chip; Jean, gin; feet, fit; seek, sick; seeks, six; sleeper, slipper; sleeps, slips; sheep, ship; meal, mill; reach, rich; leap, lip; lead, lid.
iː/eɪ	see, say; feel, fail.
iː/ɪə	bee, beer; tea, tear; see, seer; he, here.
ɪ/e	pin, pen; tin, ten; chick, check; gin, Jen; knit, net.
ɪ/ə	arches, archers; patted, pattered; potted, pottered; poaches, poachers; batted, battered; butted, buttered; buzzes, buzzers; dusty, duster; dances, dancers; catchy, catcher; catches, catchers; jury, juror; sleepy, sleeper; marches, marchers; races, racers; Lucy, looser; watches, watchers; washes, washers; wary, wearer.
ɪ/–	arty, art; penny, pen; Daddy, Dad; cosset, cost; monkey, monk; hearty, heart.
e/æ	expensive, expansive; end, and; pet, pat; pedalling, paddling; dead, Dad; Ken, can; men, man; net, gnat; head, had.
e/ɒ	jelly, jolly; pet, pot.
e/ɜː	fens, ferns.
e/eɪ	test, taste; Jen, Jane; fell, fail; sell, sail; seller, sailor; rest, raced.
æ/ʌ	batter, butter; battler, butler; banker, bunker; tracks, trucks; cap, cup;

	stamp, stump; shattered, shuttered; mashed, mushed.
æ/ɑː	cap, carp; cat, cart; had, hard.
æ/ɒ	tatter, totter; battle, bottle.
ʌ/ɑː	puck, park; buck, bark; buzz, bars; bun, barn; duck, dark; dun, darn; cup, carp; lover, larva.
ʌ/ɒ	puppy, poppy; buddy, body; bugs, bogs; ducks, docks; dun, don; suck, sock; hug, hog; wonders, wanders.
ɑː/ɒ	part, pot; tart, tot; darn, don; shark, shock; rajah, Roger; last, lost; heart, hot.
ɑː/ɜː	bard, bird; bath, birth; lark, lurk; heart, hurt.
ɑː/aʊ	art, out; bar, bow; bard, bowed; darn, down; car, cow.
ɑː/aʊə	are, our; bar, bower; tar, tower; car, cower.
ɒ/ɔː	don, dawn; cock, cork; cosset, corset; spot, sport; shot, short.
ɒ/ʊ	pot, put; box, books; cock, cook; lock, look; rock, rook.
ɒ/əʊ	off, oaf; cost, coast; John, Joan; knot, note.
ɔː/ʊ	Paul, pull; ball, bull; fall, full; fought, foot; wall, wool.
ɔː/uː	or, ooh!; Paul, pool; bought, boot; gorse, goose; fall, fool; saw, Sue; short, shoot.
ɔː/əʊ	or, oh!; Paul, pole; bought, boat; caught, coat; call, coal; called, cold; fawn, phone; fall, foal; saw, so; stalker, stoker; lord, load; a lawn, alone.
ɔː/ʊə	paw, poor; tore, tour; door, dour; bore, boor.
ʊ/uː	pull, pool; full, fool; look, Luke.
uː/ɜː	ooh!, er...; pool, pearl; ghoul, girl; juicy, jersey; Sue, sir; shoot, shirt.
uː/əʊ	ooh!, oh!; pool, pole; boot, boat; too, toe; ghoul, goal; fool, foal; Sue, so; soup, soap; shoe, show; room, Rome; ruler, roller; hoop, hope.
uː/aʊ	blues, blouse; Sue, sow; fool, fowl; shoot, shout.
uː/ʊə	two, tour; do, dour; shoe, sure.
ɜː/əʊ	er..., oh!; earth, oath; pearl, pole; birth, both; curl, coal; girl, goal; jerk, joke; fern, phone; flirt, float; sir, so; weren't, won't.
ə/–	Anna, Anne; apart, part; across, cross; aground, ground; asleep, sleep; allure, lure; poacher, poach; banker, bank; bather, bathe; totter, tot; Dinah, dine; Philippa, Philip; visitor, visit; singer, sing; seller, sell; sailor, sail; cyder, side; rollers, rolls; ladders, lads.
eɪ/aɪ	ace, ice; paper, piper; pain, pine; bait, bite; tray, try; day, die; Kate, kite; fail, file; lay, lie; lake, like; hate, height; way, why; wait, white.
eɪ/ɔɪ	Kate, quoit; chase, choice; fail, foil; sail, soil.
eɪ/əʊ	bait, boat; daisy, dozy; Kate, coat; gate, goat; grey, grow; Jane, Joan; Jane's, Jones; fail, foal; they, though; say, so; rail, roll; lay, low; wake, woke.
eɪ/ɛə	they, their; may, mare; lays, lairs; ways, wears.
aɪ/aɪə	tie, tyre; tied, tired; spy, spire; lie, liar; line, lion; high, higher; why, wire.
aɪ/ɔɪ	pies, poise; pint, point; by, boy; goodbye, good boy; tie, toy; kite, quoit; file, foil.

aɪ/aʊ	by, bow; dine, down; find, found; file, fowl; signed, sound; rise, rouse; lied, loud.
aɪə/aʊə	tyre, tower; flyer, flower; shyer, shower; highered, Howard.
ɔɪ/əʊ	boy, bow; toy, toe; quoit, coat; Joy, Joe; foil, foal; noise, nose; Roy, row; royal, roll; Hoyle, hole.
əʊ/aʊ	bow, bow; coal, cowl; cold, cowled; phoned, found; foal, fowl; sow, sow; row, row; rose, rouse; load, loud; hole, howl.
aʊ/aʊə	bow, bower; cow, cower; cowed, coward; sow, sour.
ɪə/ɛə	ear, heir; peer, pair; beer, bear; tear, tear; cheer, chair; fear, fair; rear, rare; leer, lair; here, hair; weary, wary.
p/b	pig, big; pack, back; puck, buck; park, bark; path, bath; poppy, bobby; Paul, ball; pull, bull; pie, by; peer, beer; pair, bear; pray, bray; rope, robe.
p/t	pin, tin; pen, ten; puff, tough; pot, tot; pork, talk; Paul, tall; pie, tie; peer, tear; pair, tear; poor, tour; pray, tray; top, tot; cap, cat; carp, cart; sheep, sheet; reports, retorts; harp, heart.
p/k	pat, cat; pork, cork; pearls, curls; pole, coal; pair, care; proud, crowd; tape, take; trap, track; shop, shock; yap, yak.
p/f	pin, Finn; pence, fence; pens, fens; pat, fat; palm, farm; paw, four; Paul, fall; put, foot; pull, full; pool, fool; pine, fine; pole, foal; pound, found; plait, flat; carp, calf; leap, leaf; harp, half; hoop, hoof.
p/h	pens, hens; pat, hat; pack, hack; pork, hawk; pie, high; pound, hound; peer, here; pair, hair.
p/–	pin, in; pat, at; palm, arm; paw, or; Paul, all; pearl, earl; pies, eyes; pair, heir; play, lay; thump, thumb; soup, Sue; soap, so; spoil, soil; spear, seer; sheep, she; rope, row; weep, we.
b/d	bank, dank; buck, duck; bun, dun; bark, dark; bobby, body; bog, dog; by, die; beer, dear; boor, door; brown, drown; robe, rode.
b/g	bun, gun; bard, guard; bait, gate; brand, grand; bray, grey.
b/f	beat, feet; bog, fog; bought, fought; bite, fight; bone, phone; bear, fair; bright, fright.
b/v	bow, vow.
b/m	beat, meat; bait, mate; bake, make; bear, mare; robe, Rome.
b/l	barge, large; bath, lath; bog, log; baboon, balloon; bake, lake; by, lie; bear, lair; robe, roll.
b/w	bee, we; big, wig; bun, one; bull, wool; bait, wait; bake, wake; by, why; bear, wear.
b/–	beat, eat; banker, anchor; bar, are; ball, all; birth, earth; bait, eight; both, oath; beer, ear; bear, heir; bring, ring; blot, lot; block, lock; robe, row.
t/d	Ted, dead; tank, dank; to, do; tie, die; toes, doze; town, down; tear, dear; tour, dour; trill, drill; putting, pudding; plate, played; mate, made; lout, loud; hat, had; white, wide.
t/k	tart, cart; talk, cork; tall, call; took, cook; take, cake; toy, coy; toast, coast; try, cry; pat, pack; but, buck; bait, bake; blot, block;

	Kate, cake; <u>stool, school</u>; mate, make; rot, rock; lot, lock; wait, wake.
t/tʃ	tin, chin; top, chop; <u>two, chew</u>; tear, cheer; tear, chair; it, itch; art, arch; <u>kitten, kitchen</u>; cat, catch; <u>what chain, watch-chain.</u>
t/θ	tin, thin; tank, thank; <u>tree, three</u>; tear, Thea; <u>tree, three</u>; apart, a path; boat, both.
t/s	tea, see; <u>Ted, said</u>; two, Sue; toil, soil; toe, sow; tear, seer; tower, sour; at, ass; trapped, traps; locked, locks; baked, bakes.
t/–	tin, in; tart, art; tear, ear; tear, heir; train, rain; pint, pine; beat, bee; bite, by; boat, bow; tent, ten; <u>quoit, coy</u>; great, grey; fleet, flee; flight, fly; sheet, she; shoot, shoe; note, no; newt, new; heat, he.
d/g	dun, gun; daisies, gazes; dodo, go-go; thud, thug.
d/dʒ	<u>dust, just</u>; <u>don, John</u>; dear, jeer; <u>bard, barge</u>; <u>head, hedge.</u>
d/θ	<u>dank, thank</u>; <u>dirty, thirty</u>; <u>dear, Thea</u>; <u>dread, thread</u>; bard, bath; bird, birth.
d/ð	<u>day, they</u>; ride, writhe.
d/z	do, zoo; seed, sees; <u>worried, worries</u>; had, has; ride, rise; <u>toad, toes</u>; hold, holes; gold, goals.
d/ʒ	rude, rouge.
d/n	Daddy, <u>Nanny</u>; dun, nun; <u>dodo, no, no!</u>; dear, near; due, new; <u>played, plane</u>; Ted, ten; crowd, crown; side, sign; lord, lawn; heads, hens; wide, wine.
d/r	dead, red; dank, rank; dun, run; dusty, rusty; docks, rocks; doom, room; doze, rose; dearly, really.
d/l	deep, leap; Dad, lad; dock, lock; dog, log; daisy, lazy; die, lie; dour, lure; food, fool; rude, rule; wed, well; wood, wool.
d/–	don, on; dies, eyes; deer, ear; <u>dread, red</u>; drear, rear; due, you; tired, tyre; toad, toe; called, call; cold, coal; gold, goal; seed, see; find, fine; <u>ringed, ring</u>; load, low.
k/g	<u>curls, girls</u>; Kate, gate; coat, goat; <u>coal, goal</u>; cold, gold; crone, grown; crowned, ground; buck, bug; <u>docks, dogs</u>; lock, <u>log.</u>
k/tʃ	<u>kick, chick</u>; care, chair; suck, such; <u>monk, munch</u>; Mark, march.
k/h	<u>cat, hat</u>; carp, harp; <u>cart, heart</u>; calf, half; cork, hawk; Kate, hate; comb, home; cold, <u>hold</u>; coward, Howard; care, hair.
k/–	cat, at; can, Anne; cup, up; Kate, eight; cage, age; <u>cold, old</u>; cowl, owl; care, heir; crusty, rusty; crockery, rockery; clear, Lear; quite, white; pork, paw; bank, bang; Duke, due; fact, fat; seek, see; <u>sink, sing</u>; milk, mill; work, were.
g/dʒ	<u>goose, juice</u>; go, Joe; jug, judge.
g/ŋ	agog, a gong; a log, along; <u>bag, bang</u>; rigging, ringing.
g/w	<u>gun, one</u>; <u>good, wood</u>; gate, wait; gave, wave; <u>guide, wide.</u>
g/–	<u>gate, eight</u>; gold, old; <u>ground, round</u>; glove, love; <u>glare, lair.</u>
tʃ/ts	<u>beach, beats</u>; <u>catch, cats.</u>
tʃ/tr	<u>cheese, trees</u>; <u>chick, trick</u>; chill, trill; chain, train.
tʃ/dʒ	<u>chin, gin</u>; <u>chill, Jill</u>; <u>choose, juice</u>; <u>chain, Jane</u>; <u>choice, Joyce</u>; cheers,

	jeers.
dʒ/dz	age, aids; hedge, heads.
dʒ/dr	Jill, drill; jug, drug.
f/v	fail, vale; fairy, vary; off, of; leaf, leave.
f/θ	Finn, thin; fought, thought; first, thirst; fear, Thea; free, three; Fred, thread; oaf, oath; reef, wreath; laugh, lath.
f/s	fell, sell; four, saw; fur, sir; fail, sail; foil, soil; found, sound; fear, seer; fairer, Sarah; a knife, an ice.
f/h	feet, heat; fens, hens; felled, held; fat, hat; fog, hog; fur, her; fire, higher; found, hound; fowl, howl; fear, here; fair, hair; fairy, hairy; few, Hugh.
f/w	fell, well; fall, wall; full, wool; fur, were; fire, wire; fine, wine; fairy, wary.
f/–	feet, eat; fit, it; fat, at; for, or; fall, all; fur, er...; fern, urn; fowl, owl; fair, heir; fly, lie; oaf, oh!; calf, car; loaf, low.
v/ð	varies, there is.
v/z	gave, gaze.
v/m	glove, glum; vice, mice; vary, Mary.
v/r	vest, rest; vain, rain; vale, rail.
v/w	vest, west; verse, worse; vale, whale; viper, wiper; vary, wary.
v/–	vice, ice; wave, way.
θ/ð	teeth, teethe; mouth, mouth; wreath, wreathe.
θ/s	thick, sick; thing, sing; thumb, sum; thong, song; path, pass; faith, face; mouth, mouse; wraith, race; youth, use.
θ/h	thug, hug.
θ/–	thin, in; Thea, ear; thrash, rash; thread, red; throw, row; earth, er...; oath, oh!; both, bow; bath, bar; teeth, tea; tooth, two; sixteenth, sixteen; youth, you.
ð/s	these, sees; they, say; there are stairs, Sarah stares.
ð/z	writhe, rise; breathe, breeze; teethe, teas; soothe, Sue's; bathe, bays.
ð/r	that, rat; though, row; there, rare.
ð/l	they, lay; though, low; there, lair.
ð/–	these, ease; that, at; though, oh!; their, heir; teethe, tea; soothe, Sue; bathe, bay.
s/z	ice, eyes; use (noun), use (verb); pence, pens; dance, darns; fence, fens; Sue, zoo; loose, lose.
s/ʃ	see, she; sips, ships; sock, shock; Sue, shoe; sow, show.
s/h	see, he; sir, her; soil, Hoyle; soap, hope; sound, hound; seer, here.
s/–	use, you; worse, were; ice, eye; Joyce, Joy; fierce, fear; beast, beat; docks, dock; coast, coat; guest, get; six, sick.
z/–	zoo, ooh!; eyes, eye; sees, sea; choose, chew; nose, no; rose, row.
ʃ/sk	shy, sky; shout, scout; sure, skua.
ʃ/sj	shoot, suit.
ʃ/–	shawl, all; shy, eye; show, oh!; shower, our; shout, out; share, heir; Welsh, well.

m/n	tempt, tent; comb, cone; sum, sun; mice, nice; warm, warn.
m/l	comb, coal; munch, lunch; Mark, lark; mast, last; Maud, lord; moose, loose; may, lay; make, lake; mare, lair; room, rule; home, hole; warm, wall.
m/w	may, way; make, wake; mare, wear.
m/–	time, tie; tramp, trap; smooth, soothe; march, arch; mice, ice; Rome, row; worm, were.
n/ŋ	garden, guarding, thin; thing; heron, herring.
n/r	nest, rest; gnat, rat; nun, run; not, rot; nose, rose; near, rear.
n/l	urn, earl; don, doll; cone, coal; chin, chill; fen, fell; faun, fall; fine, file; phone, foal; vain, vale; not, lot; near, leer; warn, wall.
n/–	bone, bow; dine, die; can't, cart; garden, guard; golden, gold; grown, grow; faun, four; fern, fur; friend, Fred; summon, summer; never, ever; hunt, hut; line, lie; lion, liar.
r/l	pray, play; proud, ploughed; grass, glass; read, lead; reef, leaf; rot, lot; rock, lock; rook, look; royal, loyal; row, low; rout, lout; rear, leer; rare, lair; heron, Helen.
r/w	rich, witch; red, wed; rest, west; wren, when; run, one; rail, whale; ride, wide; rare, wear.
r/h	red, head; rat, hat; rot, hot; rope, hope; roll, hole; round, hound; rear, here; rare, hare.
r/–	brand, band; break, bake; tree, tea; try, tie; dread, dead; drown, down; drear, dear; crock, cock; crone, cone; crowd, cowed; great, gate; grow, go; fright, fight; rich, itch; rat, at; ranker, anchor; race, ace; rise, eyes; rear, ear; rare, heir.
l/j	lot, yacht; lawn, yawn; loose, use (noun); lose, use (verb).
l/w	leap, weep; leather, weather; lawn, warn; lurk, work; lay, way; lake, wake; lie, why; liar, wire; lair, wear.
l/–	all, or; people, peep; Paul, paw; plane, pain; battler, batter; butler, butter; black, back; toil, toy; towel, tower; cowl, cow; clap, cap; goal, go; fall, four; fleet, feet; flat, fat; floor, four; slips, sips; royal, Roy; roll, row; real, rear; leave, Eve; leg, egg; ladder, adder; lasses, asses; label, able; loaf, oaf; lair, heir; Walter, water; wild, wide.
h/j	hello, yellow; help, yelp; hack, yak; hard, yard; hot, yacht; who, you.
h/w	he, we; head, wed; hawk, walk; her, were; hate, wait; high, why; higher, wire; hair, wear.
h/–	heat, eat; Helen, Ellen; Hannah, Anna; harbours, arbours; hearty, arty; hate, eight; hold, old; hear, ear; hair, heir; Hugh, you; Hugo, you go; (which, witch).
j/w	yacht, what; yawn, warn.
j/–	due, do; fuel, fool.
w/–	twin, tin; quick, kick; quite, kite; witch, itch; wall, all; were, er...; wait, eight; wear, heir.